THE BOOK OF
Ki

THE BOOK OF

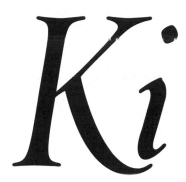

Ki

A PRACTICAL GUIDE TO
THE HEALING PRINCIPLES
OF LIFE ENERGY

MALLORY FROMM, PH.D.

PHOTOGRAPHS BY SHIRLEY BROGER AND JIM MADJID

Healing Arts Press
Rochester, Vermont

Healing Arts Press
One Park Street
Rochester, Vermont 05767
www.gotoit.com

Note to the reader: This book is intended as an informational guide. The remedies, approaches, and techniques described herein are meant to supplement, and not to be a substitute for, professional medical care or treatment. They should not be used to treat a serious ailment without prior consultation with a qualified health-care professional.

Library of Congress Cataloging-in-Publication Data
Fromm, Mallory 1949–
        The book of Ki : a practical guide to the healing principles of life energy / Mallory Fromm.
                p.   cm.
        Includes index.
        ISBN 0-89281-744-5 (pbk. : alk. paper)
        1. Ch'i kung. I. Title.
RA781.8.F76   1998   97-52080
615.8'2—dc21   CIP

Printed and bound in the United States

10 9 8 7 6 5 4 3 2 1

This book was typeset in Caslon with Throhand as the display typeface

Healing Arts Press is a division of Inner Traditions International

Distributed to the book trade in Canada by Publishers Group West (PGW), Toronto
Distributed to the health food trade in Canada by Alive Books, Toronto and Vancouver
Distributed to the book trade in the United Kingdom by Deep Books, London
Distributed to the book trade in Australia by Gemcraft Books, Burwood
Distributed to the book trade in New Zealand by Tandem Press, Auckland
Distributed to the book trade in South Africa by Alternative Books, Ferndale

Contents

Preface

This book arose from a twofold desire—first, to commemorate a master of *ki* who certainly saved my health and probably my life and, second, to cut away the obscure, even mystical way ki has hitherto been presented and provide the average Westerner with the means of creating a health program based on his or her own ki. This may be called a self-help book, but since everyone alive possesses ki, it is more a programmed guide to using what you already have than a means to attaining what you lack.

The first part of the book will take the reader through the basic rite of passage for obtaining the technique for healing and health mainte-nance through ki. The stages are these: learning to access your ki quickly and efficiently through breathing; following a series of exercises for strengthening, smoothing, and balancing your ki; and finally, learning to transmit your ki in a calming and healing way to yourself and others. As in any sport or art form, repetition is the "key." Ki is powerful, but not miraculous. It needs to be cultivated in the same way as any new field of study. However, ki will produce beneficial health results in a remarkably short period of time.

The rest of Part I is devoted to precisely how to use your ki for healing and health maintenance. Stress-related aches and pains; problems with sleep, appetite, and excretion; anxiety and stress-related psychological problems will all be dealt with. Above all, this book aims to be practical, not just placing the healing power of ki literally in the individual's hands but also showing the individual where to place his or her ki-laden hands.

Part II is a tribute to the first ki practitioner I ever met. It is meant to read as a sort of mystery with a satisfying and revealing climax. Certainly, I was mystified by her approach to health and healing, and I wish to take the reader through my early doubts and mystification to my absolute conviction in the healing power of ki and her view of health and the human body. I learned ki literally at her hands, and my subsequent years of study and practice arose from her example. She introduced me to a new world of thought and practice regarding health. It is a world at whose threshold we all stand; however, few of us are granted so much as a peek at it. We are given two aspirin and told to come back in the morning. Part II hopes to rectify this situation by presenting the world of health through ki in a vivid panorama.

In the text, I mention ki practitioners and people who are adept at using ki; these are teachers and students of ki I have trained and worked with in Japan over the past sixteen years. I owe a debt to the always obliging Toshihiko Kubota of Meiji University for his technical expertise and assistance. Finally, I offer an acknowledgment of enduring gratitude to Therese Baxter for her advice and guidance on the text and photos and for her vivid memories of our first ki practitioner.

Introduction

My illness began in 1979. I was thirty years old and living in Tokyo.

I awoke one warm Sunday morning in June and was unable to move for the keen, throbbing pain that ran from the base of my spine to the top of my left ankle. I thought reflexively of sciatica but could remember no incident or accident that might have brought it on. I had lifted nothing heavy, had received no blow, had been subject to no violent or sudden movement; nor had there been so much as a twinge hitherto that might in retrospect have been an indication of the onset of the pain. It was inexplicable. Without the use of my body I felt ghostly, insubstantial; only the local piercing pain was real and worth considering.

I had been sleeping, Japanese fashion, on the floor. Getting up was laborious, but I managed it after thirty minutes. The pain diminished as I moved about the flat and by the end of the day had lodged tenaciously in my left calf, where it stayed, to a greater or lesser degree, until I sought medical help. The feeling was constant and uncomfortable, but tolerable. I carried on with my work and routine for two weeks, more annoyed than worried, and lived with the hope that the pain would leave me as swiftly and suddenly as it had attacked me.

Two weeks after the pain began I saw two physicians in a week. The first diagnosed tendonitis and prescribed anti-inflammatory drugs. The second said I had nothing more than muscle strain and suggested hot baths, preferably mineral baths. I followed the advice of both without experiencing any change in my condition. I began to get nervous.

In September I visited an orthopedic surgeon. He was a smug, quiet man with a lachrymose style. He instructed me with a weary gesture to bend down and touch my toes. I could hardly touch my knees. He sighed, told me that I had a herniated disc resulting in sciatica of the left leg, and then had X rays taken to confirm his diagnosis. Predictably, they did. The third and fourth lumbar vertebrae had come unstuck, pushing out the cartilage between them, which was now pressing against the sciatic nerve. He prescribed total bed rest and painkillers to be taken anally, though with little confidence in either. He mentioned the possible need for a laminectomy but placed as little confidence in that procedure as he did in bed rest.

His lack of confidence was well justified. With bed rest the area of pain enlarged until it affected half the leg. The suppositories contained a steroid that left me nauseated. On my second visit he prescribed a stomach medication to counteract the side effects of the suppositories. I had a physician friend, Dr. Shibata, analyze the suppositories. He told me to throw them away, that they were harmful. The two weeks of bed rest and suppositories had diminished the pain, but by then it occupied a larger area of the calf and had become more persistent.

From September 1979 until February 1980, I tried a number of chiropractors and acupuncturists. I found the chiropractors' "adjustments" very painful and unrewarding. One dour old man, in particular, seemed to take offense that I could remember no moment of definite origin for the pain. He exacted his revenge with painful, fruitless manipulations. The acupuncturists all shared a cloying "try to be brave" expression that put me off their treatment. One practitioner was more disinterested than the rest, and I had six unsuccessful treatments from him. The three shiatsu practitioners I saw were chirpy and talkative, which helped distract me momentarily from my worry. But with no results, my worry always returned.

In June 1980, I consulted an American orthopedic surgeon in California, a young man with curly hair, a likable grin, and a rugged personality—

a backwoodsman in a white smock. Rolling up his trouser leg, he displayed a thick, disgusting gray scar running from his knee to his ankle, the legacy of a momentary lapse with a chain saw. "Now that was pain," he boasted; "what you've got is nothing." Of the dozens of health care providers I met, he was the only one to make me feel like a pantywaist. His X rays matched those of the Japanese orthopedic surgeon, and he sent me away with painkillers and an admonition to stay in bed.

I returned to Japan in September, and my situation went rapidly to pieces. Whereas hitherto the pain had been localized in the calf, with occasional forays to the toes, and lying down had provided considerable relief, the pain now ranged from my toes to my hip and raged relentlessly. No position or posture could bring relief. I began having trouble concentrating at work, and sleep was brief and unsatisfying. I became testy and anxious, the anxiety turning to fear in December, when I realized that I was losing feeling in my toes. Touching the toes produced only a sensation of cold, and a dull one at that. I had heard that this sensation was symptomatic of incipient nerve death, and, rightly or wrongly, I could not in my present condition believe other than that this was true.

I consulted another orthopedic surgeon. This one, the last, had a volatile personality tinged with hysteria. He, too, took X rays and questioned me about my lifestyle. My "failure to come to terms with my condition and give up all movement" had contributed to my wretched state of health. I should not even think of standing, much less of walking, but must take to bed for two weeks, during which time he forbade me to leave the bed. He loaned me a bedpan. Should bed rest fail, then he would put me in the hospital for two weeks of traction. If that, too, proved unsuccessful, he would be pleased to perform a laminectomy. In any case, I would be out of pain within six weeks if I submitted to his treatment.

Bed rest proved counterproductive. Friends came to care for me on a rotating schedule, but the pain grew fiercer, the toes colder. I had little appetite and hardly ate. I was becoming so physically weak that I could no longer fight against the pain. I lost hope of ever being cured and wondered if it would not be better to skip the traction and gamble on a laminectomy straightaway.

Bed rest had also become spiritually debilitating. I felt like moving—my mind and spirit were moving—but I was under orders to suppress the urge. In the end I could not. I did a little walking daily in the flat.

However, I now needed a crutch to support myself. I could no longer urinate standing up. Squeezing my stomach muscles sent bursts of pain down my leg, and I had to sit on the toilet and wait until gravity pulled the urine out of me.

In the early evening of the second Saturday of January 1981, I lapsed into a grave depression. I had no faith in orthopedic surgeons. None of the three I had seen had so much as laid a finger on me, but all relied on the evidence of X rays to provide a diagnosis. I was skeptical as to whether the X rays showed the origin of the sciatica or only its symptoms. The physicians assured me that they were one and the same, but I was not convinced. Further, all of them had prescribed bed rest, which, judging from their attitudes, was little more than a halfway house to surgery—a place to wait and wish for recovery. Yet orthopedic surgery represented one pinnacle of Western medical knowledge and technique, and as a Westerner I had a primitive urge to believe that the surgeon in his ritualistic garb and wielding the sharp scalpel of healing would not let me down. I brooded on the advisability of a laminectomy. Had my half-morbid, half-wishful state of mind continued, I may well have undergone surgery. I will never know. Okamoto's phone call came just as I had begun seriously to weigh the pros and cons.

Okamoto was a stranger to me. A friend of my close friend Patrick, Okamoto had suddenly dropped out of sight for three years until the week before. He had phoned Patrick and invited him to dinner that Saturday night. Over dinner, Okamoto reported that during the time they had not seen each other, he had suffered dreadfully from sciatica as a result of a crushing tackle while playing rugby. After following nearly the same route as I had, he had found an old woman who had healed him.

Patrick immediately gave him my phone number. Okamoto, sympathetic to a fellow sufferer, phoned me at once from the restaurant. He would make an appointment for me to see the old woman on Tuesday, he said, and offered to accompany me.

I was elated. My depression lifted, and I never thought of surgery again. This woman was a medical genius, a master of ki, a modest, compassionate woman. Her name was Kayoko Matsuura. I dedicate this book to her memory.

PART I

HEALING WITH KI

About Ki

The concept of ki pervades the fabric of daily life and thought in China and Japan. For example, the Japanese language uses ki to explain or portray a wide array of phenomena. Unlike alphabets, in which letters are selectively aligned to form a word and have no intrinsic relationship to the meaning of the word, Chinese ideograms—called *kanji* in Japanese—are the pictorial representations of words. The English word *tear* for example, meaning both "moisture in the eye" and "rip" and pronounced differently for each meaning, is impossible to reproduce using kanji. The two meanings of *tear* would each have its own kanji. Indeed, you might not know how to pronounce the kanji, but you would know the difference between the two.

The kanji for ki is found in word and phrase compounds whose meanings span the activities of life, thought, and the phenomenal world. Weather is ki; electricity is ki; air is ki; health is ki; illness is ki; purpose is ki; desire is ki; sanity and insanity are ki; feelings, both physical and emotional, are ki; getting along or not getting along with someone is due to ki; you pay attention with ki, show consideration with ki, use ki to worry as well as to remain calm. When your ki is not directed toward a certain thing, you have no inclination to do that thing. When your ki is aware of your immediate environment, you are sensitive to the feelings of others. Finally, for the purposes of this book, ki is vitality, energy, the spirit of life itself.

If ki were more demanding, it could easily set itself up as a sort of deity. After all, we are born from ki and die from ki. Fate might determine whom we meet, but it is ki that determines whom we love and whom we hate. Deities are demanding; it is necessary to show gratitude at regular intervals to demonstrate our awareness of the deity's presence. A deity with such a quiet, all-embracing nature could easily be taken for granted.

This is exactly what has happened to ki. Just as we live in and depend upon air—though we are usually unaware of it (when the air is clean)— so the average Japanese lives in an environment of ki, but hardly gives ki a thought. However, ask a Japanese to carry on a simple conversation omitting the use of the word ki, either by itself or in a compound, and you will find yourself up against a very unhappy individual. The word *tortured* might be an exaggerated adjective to apply to the person, but *frustrated* might just as easily be an understatement. There is no single word or concept in the English language remotely comparable to ki in scope, utility, and importance.

The main hurdle encountered when writing about ki for an Occidental audience is how to explain the phenomenon. It seems as remote to an American as it is commonplace to someone from Japan. Indeed, I have found two distinctly opposing reactions to the phenomenon of ki among Western audiences. The first is to scoff. Ki is unscientific and irrational and therefore does not exist. It is as silly a Chinese concept as the Taoist's Elixir of Immortality. The other reaction is to view ki as something special, even sacred. Being Eastern, it is exotic, and ranging so wide in scope, it is pregnant with meaning and potential. The former reaction seeks to close the door on ki, while the latter would lock it in a lovely scented box to remove only on special occasions.

It is possible to render ki into English as "life force," "life essence," or "vital spark." It is just as easy to render it as "electromagnetism." All of these meanings would be correct and yet somehow misleading. I prefer the word *energy*, but, as in the case of the other words, I am left dissatisfied. Each by itself is too narrow to convey the range of ki and, at the same time, fails to convey the ordinariness of ki. Moreover, the words spelled out in Roman letters leave a vague impression. A Japanese or Chinese will have a clear mental picture of ki. This is what ki looks like.

This visual relationship with ki helps make its meaning more accessible. Thus I will give a visual description of ki rather than grope for an equivalent term.

For example, if two tissue samples are taken of one person, one immediately before and the other immediately after death, both samples will appear identical under pathologic examination. It would be impossible to detect that one sample comes from a corpse. But at the moment of death, ki was terminated. The difference between life and death is the presence or absence of ki.

Every living thing has ki, which is not to say that every living thing possesses ki in equal amounts. The ki of human beings is both general and specific. It is general in that each of us has it, and its basic characteristics are universally shared. It is specific in that the degree and texture of ki differ from individual to individual. The realm of ki is in complete agreement with Freud's dictum that anatomy is destiny. The ki you are born with is the ki you will have until you die, and the qualities of that ki are, to put it simply, what make you who you are.

Some people have weak ki, while others have strong ki. (In Japanese, the former are called "weak-willed" and the latter "strong-willed.") Some people's ki seems to be positive and active, while other people's ki is tranquil and passive. I have encountered ki that is warm and invigorating; I have experienced ki that is cool and soothing. In short, there is no "proper" ki, just as there is no "proper" human being. For the ki novice, it is good to know that you may expect to encounter as many types of ki as there are types of people (which in the realm of ki is basically twelve, with a number of subtypes due to variation).

Because ki is the basis of health, it is apposite to consider just what health is from the ki point of view. There is no standard of health—ki recognizes no criteria of perfect health. Some people are naturally healthy, while others have lemon bodies from the start. I know people who believe that tobacco and alcohol are foods and who have ingested little else over a long, healthy lifetime. I know others who have become young martyrs to fitness and dietary programs, keeling over from a stroke in their thirties. Ki makes absolutely no claims to making a person healthy. The presence of strong ki can make a person *as healthy as that person is physiologically able to be.*

If ki has a philosophy of health it is this: Health is the satisfaction one takes in life. If drinking and smoking give you more pleasure than anything else and you have considered the consequences, then ki will not forbid you to drink or smoke. It would prefer that you didn't, but where living is concerned, ki prefers quality to quantity. Ki awards no prizes for longevity. It prizes a vigorous appreciation of living.

It is also good to be advised from the outset that your ki will not mesh with the ki of everyone you encounter. Just as you take to some people and not to others, so your ki will harmonize wonderfully with some and be unreceptive to others. Some people's ki will actually repel your own, making them impregnable to your touch. Such extreme cases of two ki forces not getting along are rare, but they do exist. Generally, it is possible to make slow and steady inroads into even unreceptive ki. Be prepared to find some people absorbing your ki with such ease and speed that it seems to be sucked out of you; at the same time, you may also expect to encounter people who receive your ki grudgingly, if at all.

It is never good to force ki on anyone. In other words, ki is not a party trick that will always produce surprisingly beneficial results. The recipient must actively want ki, or treatment may produce unpleasant side effects. You cannot hurt anyone with ki in the sense of leaving a lasting or lingering effect. However, a feeling of discomfort, nausea, or even anxiety may occur if the ki of the recipient does not welcome that of the provider.

The fact that each of us possesses ki from the moment of conception until the moment of death does not make it easier to use our ki well, just as the fact that we have a voice does not entitle us to sing at Carnegie Hall. Ki has to be trained. To put it another way, we have to sensitize ourselves to the extent that we are able to feel and use ki with delicacy and precision. It is the sensitizing of our bodies and senses that is the most difficult and time-consuming part of ki training. Ninety-eight of

100 people are able to access their ki and transmit it to someone else within an hour of beginning to learn the technique. However, to feel ki working within you and working within someone else (as opposed to seeing the healing results of your ki) takes years of giving and receiving ki.

It should be an effortless, even natural matter to be aware of ki. However, there is another, just as powerful logic that desensitizes us and makes ki training a necessity. The human mind and body shift constantly between tension and relaxation. We tense when we inhale and relax when we exhale. All movement is based on alternating tension and relaxation. Our internal organs, too, are in this state of flux.

Tension keeps us alert and sharp; relaxation makes us calm and sensitive. The pace, direction, needs, and goals of our lives force us into a situation in which tension gains the upper hand and relaxation ceases to play a major role. Sometimes relaxation becomes so marginal as to hardly exist, which accounts for stiff necks and shoulders, headaches, eyestrain, lower-back pain, and a range of other aches and ailments. We have lost the balance between tension and relaxation and become desensitized. William Blake understood the phenomenon very well when he wrote (in "Proverbs of Hell"), "Damn braces; bless relaxes." Most of us are damned to a life of discomfort through tension. Ki can be a blessing for us.

A number of other factors work to desensitize us for our own good. Given the pace of our lives and the quantity of stimuli we encounter willy-nilly during our waking hours, we would no doubt experience sensory overload if we retained our natural sensitivity. We have, through technology, removed ourselves so far from nature that to have a naturally sensitive body would kill us. We cool our environment in summer and warm it in winter. I go from my air-conditioned house to my air-conditioned car to my air-conditioned office and back again, hardly knowing that the temperature is 104 degrees. I live and work in an environment of 72 degrees throughout the year. My food is no longer seasonal. Battery farming, fish farms, hothouses, the entire Southern Hemisphere, refrigeration, genetic alteration, and modern packaging provide me with a constant, unvaried diet. My body hardly experiences seasonal changes, and when it does, I become alarmed and seek medical attention.

Ki training and sensitization simply restore the balance of tension and relaxation. Ki puts tension where there is a deficiency and induces relaxation where there is a deficiency. Practically speaking, since all of us are inclined to tension, ki training and practice are therefore relaxation techniques. For those rare people who suffer from an excess of relaxation, ki training and practice will provide the necessary tension.

I mentioned the human mind and body. Unlike the Chinese and Japanese languages, English discriminates between the two. It is possible using kanji 心 身 to show mind and body as a unity. I wish to stress this because it is of the essence when experiencing ki. Ki admits no distinction between mind and body. You cannot tie a shoelace without a mind, no matter how feeble, any more than you can do mathematical calculations without a body, no matter how feeble. Using ki for health maintenance and healing is always premised on the mind-body unity. Just as sensitivity comes from a balance of tension and relaxation, health derives as much from mental as physical factors and must always be taken into account when giving ki.

Finally, in our age of limits and finite resources, it is reassuring to know that ki is inexhaustible. Ki is like Cleopatra's beauty; it feeds off itself and continues ever increasing. The more you actively use and transmit your ki, the more ki you will have to use and transmit. An ability to use ki to your full potential is best described in Blake's words from "Proverbs of Hell": "Energy is eternal delight."

In short, ki is a type of energy that informs all living matter. It is subject to external stimuli, such as other ki, changes in the weather, or an accident. It responds to internal stimuli such as anxiety and stress. When your ki is "gloomy," you are depressed and listless. When your ki is "pristine," you feel like a million bucks.

Ki will not make you prettier, slimmer, or more muscular, but it will make you more energetic, more concentrated, and more relaxed. An ability to concentrate ki effortlessly is invigorating. You find yourself with the energy and enthusiasm you had in childhood. You can accomplish tasks with less wasted energy and in a shorter period of time. And best of all, you will have both the inclination and ability to maintain the health of yourself and your family.

Accessing Your Ki

Instructions for accessing one's own ki will strike the novice as somewhat labored. However, once you have experienced the feeling of your own ki, the procedure becomes more simple. After a few weeks, accessing your ki will be as routine as brushing your teeth, and the step-by-step procedure described here may be abbreviated to suit your taste.

A calm, peaceful environment is always recommended, especially for the beginner. An experienced person can get in touch with ki in almost any environment, but since concentration is of the essence, noise-free surroundings are preferred.

Sit on a firm seat with both feet squarely on the floor. A backless seat, such as a low stool or piano bench, is preferable. People have a tendency to lean back and let the chair support their backs; a backless seat will ensure that you are supporting your spine. (Those who aspire to Oriental authenticity may sit on their knees. This posture ensures that the lower spine is strong and supporting the head; however, for most Westerners, the ensuing discomfort from loss of feeling in the lower legs diminishes the ability to relax and concentrate.)

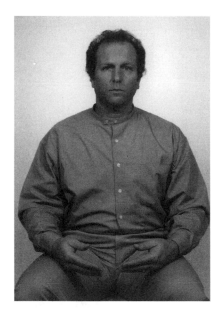

Figure 1

Sit erect, but without tension. Consciously align your head with your spinal cord so that the small of your back takes the weight of your head. Let your hands find a natural and comfortable position on your lap (figure 1). Many people feel most comfortable with their forearms on their laps. Be aware of your breathing and of tension in your solar plexus. Note that by slowing or deepening your breathing you can relax your solar plexus. Most people's breathing is shallow during their waking hours, a sign of tension. Our breathing slows and deepens when we sleep; those whose breathing remains shallow during sleep are unable to enjoy a deep sleep.

Before beginning to access your ki, give yourself half a minute to calm down and become aware of your breathing. The ideal kind of breathing for these exercises is the archetypal first breath taken at the beginning of a vacation. You get out of your car at the seaside or in the mountains, fill your lungs with fresh air, and then exhale slowly and sensually, enjoying the act of breathing. It's a hackneyed cinematic image, with the breather exclaiming, "Now that's what I call air!" However, that is the sort of deep, slow breathing required to gain the full benefit of these exercises.

Do not overdo deep breathing. Just breathe as deeply as you feel comfortable doing. If your breathing causes stress or discomfort, reduce your air intake to a natural, comfortable level.

You may also want to change the direction in which you are sitting to relax your solar plexus. The more relaxed your solar plexus, the faster you will access your ki. *Breathe slowly through the nose until told otherwise.* You are now ready to begin.

Standard Procedure

Raise your hands to the level of your mouth, keeping them six inches apart and about six to eight inches from your body. Your hands should assume a natural curved shape. Your elbows should be slightly splayed and pointing downward (figure 2).

At the start, it is necessary to visualize your ki. I recommend that you imagine ki as a white vapor, like steam. *Breathing through the mouth,* send a steady, gentle stream of air between your hands. Imagine the air to be a white vapor. See it fill the space between your hands as you feel its coolness on your palms. After three exhalations, imagine that the vapor has coalesced into a ball-shaped mass between your two hands.

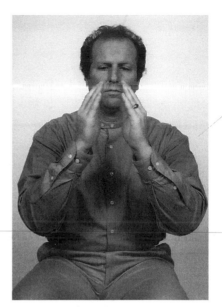

Figure 2

Begin to play with the ball. Move your hands slowly and gently out and in, watching the ball expand and contract. Keep exhaling lightly between your hands so that the physical feeling confirms the changing visual shape (figure 3a).

In about twenty seconds you will feel that your hands have an attraction for each other, a feeling like weak magnetism. As you move your hands back and forth, you will find that they are drawn together and that the size of the vapor ball will diminish. Your hands will draw closer and closer together, but do not let them touch until you feel that they are strongly drawn to each other (figure 3b). Then, very gently, let your hands come together. The vapor will be pushed out from between them and scatter into the air.

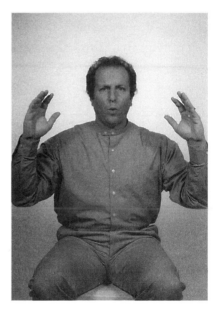

Figure 3a

Figure 3b

Figure 4

Begin breathing slowly through the nose again. Your hands will now have assumed an attitude of prayer (figure 4). Your fingers and the heels of your palms should be touching. The more the hands touch, the faster you can access your ki, but the hands should be relaxed and you should not force your hands to flatten together.

Feel for tension in your shoulders. If they are raised too high, let them drop gently until you feel relaxed. Your hands will be chest high, and the fingertips will usually be pointing away from you. Close your eyes gently (figure 5). Once again visualize your breath as a white vapor.

Inhale through your fingertips. This means that when you inhale through your nose, you imagine the air entering your body as a white vapor coming into your hands through your fingertips and traveling down your arms until it reaches your elbows. *Feel* the air travel through your palms and down the arms to the elbows.

On the exhale, see and feel the white vapor travel up from your elbows to your hands and then out through your fingertips. As you continue this gentle breathing, feel the air coming in cool from the outside and leaving your body warm.

Keep up a rhythmic breathing through the nose, and after a minute you will feel your palms begin to tingle slightly. As you continue your breathing and visualization, the tingling sensation will spread to your fingers. You will feel that in addition to your breath leaving your fingertips, there is a steady wavelike force traveling out of you through your hands. You have accessed your ki. If someone stands beside you and puts a hand, palm down, about six inches over your fingertips, they will feel the wavelike flow (figure 6). Ki does not flow from the body only on the exhale. It is a constant flow. There is no need to push or strain your exhalation to make more ki flow out. In fact, straining will produce the opposite effect. The more rhythmic, natural, and deep the breathing, the greater the outflow of ki.

Continue your breathing until your hands are entirely warm and tingling. I recommend *three to five minutes*. The sensation is so pleasurable that many people will carry on for seven to ten minutes.

In order to maintain your ki in a central location rather than have it diffuse throughout your body, end this procedure in the following way.

When you are ready to stop, take a deep breath *through the nose* and swallow it. You should feel tension suddenly return to your solar

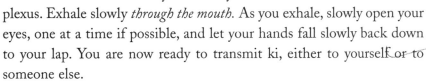

Figure 5

plexus. Exhale slowly *through the mouth.* As you exhale, slowly open your eyes, one at a time if possible, and let your hands fall slowly back down to your lap. You are now ready to transmit ki, either to yourself or to someone else.

After three or four experiences of accessing your ki, you may begin to shorten the procedure. Visualization of the white vapor is usually the first step to be omitted, and the time needed for the hands to be drawn naturally together decreases to only ten or twenty seconds. You may no

longer feel like having your breath travel as far as your elbows; instead you may prefer to keep it longer in your palms. Experimentation will lead to modification. What is important to remember when accessing your ki is to be aware of tension or relaxation in your solar plexus and to keep your breathing steady and gentle. Also, it is not

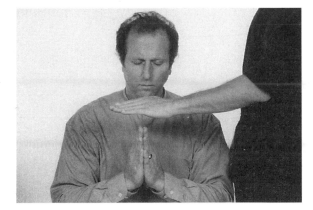

Figure 6

at all necessary to be anatomically correct when visualizing or feeling the air moving through your fingertips and down to your elbows. Simply imagine it, and you will feel it.

Advanced Procedure

Breathe slowly through the nose throughout this procedure.

Figure 7

Seat yourself as you would for the standard procedure. Place the three middle fingers (forefinger, middle finger, ring finger) of each hand on either side of the solar plexus (figure 7). Feel gently for tension. Turn your entire body to face different directions until you face the direction where the solar plexus is most relaxed.

Having changed your position to find the direction in which you are most comfortable, place your hands together as in the standard procedure (figure 5). Raise your hands so that the thumbs are at the level of your eyes and pointing at them. You will feel tension in your solar plexus. Relax your shoulders suddenly so that your hands fall to a position somewhere in front of you. Most people's hands naturally fall to about the level of the breastbone (figure 8).

Close your eyes slowly and gently. Inhale deeply through the nose and swallow the air. Feel the tension in your solar plexus. Exhale slowly *through the palms and out the fingertips.*

Once again, it is a good idea to visualize the air you inhale and exhale as a white vapor. Inhale the vapor through your fingertips and palms into the *small of the back.*

It is not necessary for the vapor to follow an anatomically correct route. Simply see and feel the vapor go straight through your body from the fingertips into the palms, down to the wrists, and from the wrists to the small of the back. Specifically, your breath should go to the *third and fourth lumbar vertebrae.*

The third lumbar vertebra (L3) is located directly behind the navel. To find L4, place your hands on your hips. Move your hands slowly upward until they find the top of your pelvis. Trace a line with your

Figure 8

thumbs from the top of the pelvis to the small of the back, and your thumbs will stop at L4. This area should receive your breath (figure 9).

Figure 9

At first, breathing into the L3 and L4 vertebrae gives a cool, even cold sensation. Some people actually shiver. When you feel that your breath has filled the L3 and L4 area, exhale slowly, following the same route as the inhalation. After half a dozen breaths, you will feel your L3 and L4 vertebrae expand and contract as if they are fulfilling the role of the lungs. Soon your palms and then your fingers will tingle, and ki will be streaming out of your hands in a wavelike flow. Continue this breathing for three to five minutes.

While engaged in this procedure, most people's heads will naturally incline slightly forward. Consciously raise your head so that the neck is straight and the spinal cord is supporting the head.

To end this procedure, breathe deeply through your fingers until you cannot hold any more air. Swallow the breath and be aware of the tension in your solar plexus. Exhale slowly *through the mouth*. Open your eyes slowly, one at a time if possible, and let your hands open and fall slowly and naturally to your lap. At the end of the exhalation, you should feel very relaxed, and your hands should feel warm. You are now ready to transmit ki.

This procedure is faster and more efficient than the standard one. However, it requires a certain level of experience to master.

Many people stymie themselves by visualizing the white vapor reaching the L3 and L4 vertebrae along an anatomically correct route—through the fingers, palms, wrists, and elbows up to the shoulders, across the clavicle to the spinal cord, and then down to the base of the spine. If this route is a convenient aid for learning or experiencing the technique, that is well and good. However, breath and ki can cut right through the body in the shortest route you can imagine. *The essence of this advanced procedure is to maintain a breathing connection between the hands and the lower spine.*

Ki Training Exercises

Ki training exercises have two fundamental goals: the first is, of course, to strengthen your ki, and the second is to sensitize you to the giving and receiving of ki.

Most ki training requires at least two people, the giver and the receiver. It is good to train with more than one other person in order to experience different types of ki and different degrees of sensitivity. Sensitivity depends upon relaxation, so all participants in ki training exercises should first access their ki. The following are standard training exercises regularly performed by all ki practitioners, no matter how proficient.

Sitting Exercises

Both people should sit on the same type of seats used in the exercises, or sit on their knees on the floor, Japanese-style.

The giver and receiver should be seated about three feet apart, the receiver positioned in silhouette. The giver will make a "gun" out of the right hand, with the thumb as the cock, and the forefinger and middle finger making the barrel. The arm should be straight, keeping the elbow gently bent.

The receiver should close his or her eyes and hold out the left arm, with the palm facing the giver, in a comfortable position. This becomes the target (figure 10).

1

The giver's "ki gun" should be about six inches from the middle of the receiver's palm. The giver's eyes may be open or closed, whichever is more conducive to concentration. The giver takes a deep, slow breath *through the nose* and exhales *through the barrel of the gun.* Ki will begin to stream out from the two fingers. Con-

Figure 10

tinue breathing in this way. Although you inhale through the nose and exhale through the fingers, *your ki will continuously stream out, even during inhalation.* Ki is not present in exhalation only; it is just as strong on inhalation.

At this point, the beginner may experience difficulty in concentrating. At the start of ki training exercises, I recommend the beginner say something *internally.* It is best to repeat over and over a positive idea to yourself, phrases such as "I am sending out ki" or "My ki is leaving my body." More specifically, one can say, "I am sending ki out through my fingers into the receiver's hand" or "The ki from my fingers is going directly into the receiver's palm." Repeating such phrases within will not just aid in concentration, it will also focus and strengthen the outflowing ki. When your partner informs you that the ki is being received, it should give you the confidence to give up repeating the mantra.

Within thirty seconds to a minute, the receiver should be aware of a sensation on the palm. It may be as gentle as a puff of wind touching the palm. It may be a warm or cool pulsating feeling. It may feel simply like heat or cold. The most common sensation is that of a feather lightly tickling the area.

If, after two minutes, the receiver still has not felt anything, do not worry. It means one of two things—the giver's ki is weak or else it is not coming out (due to lack of proper concentration), in which case the accessing procedure should be repeated. However, this circumstance is rare. More commonly, it stems from a lack of sensitivity on the part of the receiver. In this case, it is good to try the exercise over again, this time the giver using the left hand and the receiver the right.

Assuming that the receiver begins to feel the ki, have the person describe the quality of the ki. Commonly used adjectives (in Japanese) are *tranquil, placid, rough, sharp, strong, gentle, warm, hot, cool, tepid, intense,* and *diffuse.* Colors are also used to describe ki. The ki that most people enjoy and respond to best is described as transparent. In other words, it has no color or dominant characteristic, just a continuously pleasurable sensation.

It is also important for the receiver to inform the giver of any change in strength or sensation of the ki. The purpose of the exercise is to project a strong, *steady* stream of ki.

When the receiver senses your ki from six inches away, slowly draw your hand back to eight inches and project your ki from there. Next withdraw to ten inches. If at this distance your ki is still being strongly and steadily felt, it is time to end the exercise. This exercise generally lasts *four to five minutes* for each hand. However, *feel free to end the exercise whenever you like.*

In the case of ki training exercises, you may end simply by lowering your gun and having your partner open her eyes. I recommend that you keep your ki centered at the end by inhaling deeply through the nose, swallowing, and then exhaling slowly *through the mouth* as you lower your gun.

Partners should now change roles and then reverse again, this time using the other hand. Once you are able to project your ki strongly and steadily at a distance of ten inches, it is time to move to the next step. (This assumes that you and your partner are sensitive to receiving ki. If not, there is no point in moving on to the next step.)

2

The relative positions of the giver and receiver are the same. The eyes of the receiver must be closed, while the eyes of the giver must be open. The giver aims the ki gun *carefully* at a particular place on the receiver's hand. It may be the tip of the middle finger, it may be the second joint on the little finger, or it may be where the forefinger meets the palm. It is good for the giver to repeat internally the point at which he is aiming during this exercise, for example: "I am sending ki to the callus at the base of the middle finger" or "I am shooting ki at the fleshy part of the palm below the thumb." The receiver should, within thirty seconds to a minute, be able to tell you where you are aiming your ki. Whether or not the receiver senses the location correctly, change your aim to another part of the hand. Aim at a total of three different points.

3

It is more difficult, but extremely interesting, to use your ki gun to draw a number on the palm of the hand. This must be done very slowly, and the receiver must be relaxed and focusing concentration on the palm. With regular practice, within three months you should be able to draw numbers (letters are difficult, but not impossible, to read) on a sensitive person's palm and have them read by the receiver.

This exercise usually takes longer than the preceding two and is also a little more strenuous for both the giver and the receiver. For this reason, it is best to limit this exercise to ten minutes. When both giver and receiver succeed in projecting and reading numbers with both left and right hands within two minutes of commencing the exercise, they have reached the stage where they should begin the advanced procedure for accessing ki. *The ability to read ki is just as important as the ability to project it.*

4

For this exercise, a long, slender, pointed object is needed. A sharpened pencil, a pen, a screwdriver, scissors, or a small knife such as a steak knife will do. For the purpose of this explanation, I will assume that the object

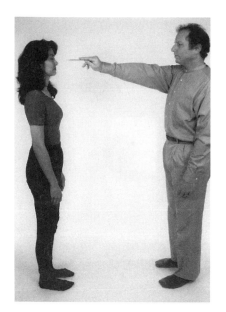

Figure 11

is a sharpened pencil. Many people engaged in ki training exercises feel that the ki from the gun is too diffuse and wish to concentrate it. In this exercise, the ki will be projected from the tip of the pencil. For those people who wish to visualize during this exercise, the ki from the gun may be compared to the beam of a flashlight, broad and diffuse, while the ki from the tip of the pencil is like the beam of a laser, intense and concentrated.

Hold the pencil close to the end lightly, but firmly with the thumb, forefinger, and middle finger of either hand. The giver and receiver should be standing or seated comfortably about *five to six feet apart,* facing each other. The *receiver's eyes* should be *closed,* and those of the *giver* should be open. The giver should *completely straighten* and raise one arm and level it like a rifle at the receiver's face. The giver aims the ki rifle (the tip of the pencil) at some small part of the receiver's face (figure 11).

Using the same technique as in Exercise 1, project ki down the length of your arm, through your three fingers, and into the pencil. *Feel your ki converge from your three fingers into the narrow shaft of the pencil.* Visualize your ki as a laser beam of white light racing from the sharp tip of the pencil to the point at which you are aiming on the receiver's face. As you do this, you may repeat internally a phrase such as "I am sending a laser beam of ki down my arm and through the tip of the pencil to hit her on the tip of the nose" or "I am sending a steady stream of ki to the center of the receiver's forehead."

Remember *your ki is not linked only to your exhalation but flows out in a continuous, steady stream.* It is good to move the tip of the pencil slightly up and down or back and forth as if tickling the area. *Do not move the pencil with your fingers, but instead move your entire arm from the shoulder.* When you feel that your ki is reaching the part of the face at which you are aiming, ask the receiver to tell you if or where the ki is felt. Some beginners are naturals and give and receive ki with ease. Most, however, have difficulty sensing ki directed to the face. Do not be discouraged if the receiver does not feel your ki the first or second time you attempt this exercise.

When the receiver answers correctly (in other words, senses where your ki is landing), increase the distance between you gradually until the tip of the rifle is *eight feet* from the receiver's face. One sure sign of strong, steady ki is the ability to give the receiver an itchy nose or even make the person sneeze by tickling the tip of the nose with your ki. When you are able to do this with both the left and right hands, you will know you have developed to a high level of ability.

Note that it is both fun and beneficial to practice this technique on a receiver's head, that is, the face, side, and back of the head. I do not, however, recommend that you attempt this exercise on a receiver's neck or chest. Only ki adepts will be able to sense ki in this area, and the giver tends to become tired and discouraged.

Before proceeding to the final sitting exercise for partners, it is timely to mention one more thing about the nature of ki, touched on in the first chapter. The strength, texture, and feel of one's ki at any given time is largely determined by how one is feeling at that time. If you have worries when projecting ki, your ki will reflect those worries. If you are agitated about something, your ki will literally feel agitated to a receiver. If you are calm and warmhearted, your ki will be soothing and tranquilizing to a receiver.

Most human animals do not easily sense this character of ki—they have become desensitized for reasons given in the first chapter. Other animals, however, are extremely sensitive to the character and texture of ki at any given time. Exercise 4 is the ultimate seated ki partner training exercise. If you are able to do it, you will be in no doubt as to the character of your ki (and, therefore, your true state of mind) at the time you project your ki.

5

Many people have pets. For those who do not, find a friend with a pet, and borrow it for a few minutes. This exercise can be done with either a cat or a dog. I have found cats to be more sensitive (meaning that they are faster to respond) than dogs. I will, therefore, use a cat for my example in this exercise. Access your ki. Sit in a comfortable position anywhere you like, on a couch or an easy chair—anywhere you and the cat feel relaxed. It may be necessary for you to slouch somewhat in order to hold the cat on your lap, but it is better to keep your back straight.

Seat the cat on your lap. Whether it is asleep or awake or in that drowsy, twilight cat world does not matter. Place one hand lightly on the cat's back so that your palm lies on the spinal cord. The hand may be either vertical or horizontal to the spine; the horizontal position is usually easier to maintain and more comfortable for the human. It does not matter where on the spine you place your hand. You may put it on the cat's head, but many cats feel uncomfortable with the weight. Looking at your hand, *inhale deeply and silently through the nose and exhale through the full palm.* There is no need to visualize a route for your breath. Simply imagine it leaving your palm and entering the cat's spine. Keep breathing this way in a slow, natural rhythm.

The cat will feel the ki by your second exhalation. Usually, the cat will twitch to show that it has sensed the ki.

Now comes the interesting part. If the ki is arrhythmic, agitated, abrupt, or unsteady, the cat will make its displeasure known at once. I have seen cats react by bristling and snarling. Their fur stands on end. Most cats react to the discomfort with a small shriek, jump off your lap, and rush out of the room. If the ki is soothing and steady, the cat will begin purring loudly almost at once and fall into what appears to be a coma. Should a cat react with displeasure to your ki, it does not mean that there is anything wrong with your ki. It should be taken as an indication of your state of mind at that moment.

I do ki training with my cat, Basil, almost every night before bed. Because he reacts with supreme displeasure to any agitation or disturbance in my ki, I put myself into a relaxed state of mind before practicing on him. The exercise soothes the two of us, and we both sleep the better for it. I know an extremely adept and eccentric ki practitioner who practices on fish. He puts his hand into his aquarium and consciously sends ki through the water into his goldfish. He claims it tranquilizes them and slows them down. I have never witnessed him doing this and, having no aquarium of my own (thanks to Basil), report this merely as an interesting field for investigation and experimentation.

Standing Exercise

This exercise is similar to Exercise 4. The giver will use a pointed object as a rifle. The receiver should stand with his back toward the giver. The eyes may be open or closed. Some people find it difficult to remain standing comfortably with their eyes closed. The giver should be about *seven feet* from the receiver. Holding the rifle as in the previous exercise, straighten your arm and raise it so that it is aiming at a single vertebra along the receiver's spine. The tip of your rifle will be a little less than *six feet* from the receiver's back.

It is not necessary to know precisely the number of the vertebra, though it might help. (There are seven cervicals, twelve thoracics, five lumbars, five sacral, and four coccygeals, and each has a number counted in sequence from the head down. You may consult the Reference for Locating Points, pp. 36–37.) Visualize your ki rifle sending a laser beam into one vertebra rather than over a wide area. If possible, imagine the receiver's spine superimposed on his shirt. *Wearing a shirt does not interfere with the passage of ki.* The result will be the same whether the receiver is naked or wearing a fur coat. Ki passes through even the thickest clothes.

Project your ki out of your rifle while repeating internally a positive phrase such as "I am sending a strong stream of ki into that vertebra just between the shoulder blades," "My ki is hitting that vertebra right behind the navel," or "My ki is entering the vertebra just below the neck." When you feel that your ki has successfully penetrated that vertebra, ask the receiver to touch the vertebra where he feels the ki. In the beginning, it should take the receiver about *sixty to ninety seconds* to feel the ki. Should the receiver be able to identify correctly the vertebra aimed at even two out of five times, both giver and receiver have strong ki and good sensitivity. Should the receiver initially be unable to identify the correct vertebra even one time out of ten, there is no reason for disappointment.

This exercise is very important and very difficult. *The spine is the seat of relaxation and well-being,* yet most of us have tense, insensitive, and unreceptive spinal cords. Our physical traumas, neuroses, and tension resulting from external stress all come to lodge in the spine. Most people have poor posture whether they are sitting or standing, which is another burden for the spine to bear. Fitness programs, too, tend to upset the balance of tension in the spine. Most produce weakness in the lumbar vertebrae and excessive tension in the upper dorsal vertebrae.

It takes months of practice in accessing ki and months of basic ki training before a receiver is able to sense ki in individual vertebrae. To be able to do this may be regarded as a fine achievement on the road to giving and receiving ki. For this reason, neither the giver nor the receiver should feel discouraged if early on there is an inability to sense ki in the spine. It is important to continue your ki training until you are able to do this exercise well. The following two exercises will help you sensitize your spine. They may be performed while sitting or standing. In the case of the second exercise, I recommend the beginner first attempt it from the sitting position.

Solitary Exercises

1

The goal of this exercise is to impart a sense of balance between your hands for transferring ki. It will also make you aware of changing tension and relaxation in your spine. This awareness is the first step toward gaining sensitivity.

You will need two objects of different size, shape, and weight, for example, a round glass paperweight and a box of tissues or a magazine and a pair of reading glasses. Anything will do. For the sake of this explanation, I will use two cups of different size.

Sit or stand comfortably. Be aware of your breathing and of the degree of tension in your solar plexus. Keeping your upper arms at your sides, raise your hands—elbows bent and palms up—to a natural and comfortable height. Having found this comfortable position, either you yourself grasp or have someone lay one object on each upturned palm. One object will feel quite a bit heavier than the other. You will also be aware of a difference in texture between them.

Gently close your eyes. Begin breathing slowly *through the nose*. No special visualization is required. This is normal, calm breathing. Be aware of your breath

Figure 12

for a few seconds, and then shift your awareness back to the objects lying on your palms.

Move your arms to different positions as you continue your breathing (figure 12). One may go up, and the other may go out, one may go down, and the other may go away from you. With each change of position, first be aware of any change in the feeling of weight between the objects. Next, be aware of changes in the areas of tension and relaxation in your spine. Feel your spine move as you slowly move your arms, and feel tension shift from vertebra to vertebra.

You may change your position to face another direction as well as move your arms during this exercise. *You will find a combination of direction and hand position in which the weight of the two objects feels the same.* In other words, you will be able to distinguish between the two objects only by their different shapes and textures.

When you have achieved the feeling of balance, inhale deeply through the nose, swallow your breath, and exhale slowly through the nose. Continue breathing normally.

At this point you should feel a unity between your two hands and your spine, especially on your exhalation. You should not be aware of three objects doing three different things but of one organism in balance. *You will soon lose awareness of the objects on your palms.* When it takes a conscious effort to feel the objects, end the exercise simply by opening your eyes and putting down the objects in your hands. I do not recommend doing this exercise for more than *six minutes* at a time. If you are initially unable to find a feeling of balance between the objects, rest for a while before trying again.

2

This exercise is perhaps the most difficult of all. It is also the most rewarding. The goal is the relaxation of the spine and from there the relaxation of the entire organism, including the mind. This exercise may be performed sitting or standing, but as I wrote earlier, the beginner should attempt to do it while seated.

Sit on a firm seat, preferably without a back. (Sitting on the knees on the floor is also fine.) Have both feet planted on the floor. Your arms may be hanging at your sides, or you may lay your hands on your lap, whichever is more comfortable.

Your head should be aligned with your spinal cord.

Imagine your spine going straight up and out through the crown of your head. With two fingers, gently feel that exit spot on your crown

Figure 13

(figure 13). When you touch the spot, be aware of the sensation and the location. Gently close your eyes. Inhale deeply through the nose, swallow the breath, and then exhale slowly through the nose. On your next breath, *inhale through the exit spot on your crown.* In order to do this, you should visualize a nebulous cool white vapor hovering just over the spot. When you inhale, the vapor is sucked into the spot. Imagine the white vapor traveling slowly down the entire length of your spine.

Be aware of your spine terminating on the firm seat. When the white vapor reaches the end of your spinal cord, it exits the tubelike spinal cord and fills the large cavity where the base of the spine meets the seat.

When you exhale, imagine the vapor being sucked up into the tube-like spinal cord and moving slowly upward until it passes out of your head at the exit spot. There it hovers until you take your next breath.

On your next inhalation, feel the coolness of the white vapor and see it travel down the spinal column. Feel the coolness collect in the cavity at the base of the spine.

After about thirty seconds, the base of your spine should feel cool while, at the same time, you may sweat from the scalp or forehead. *This is not only normal but also desirable.* As you continue breathing, feel the rhythm of your breathing, the steady, endless flow of air up and down your spine.

If it is possible, visualize the white vapor passing down the spine from vertebra to vertebra. Imagine a side view of your spinal cord, with the white vapor passing down each vertebra and then back up again. You will feel the spinal cord relax. Do not be surprised if you feel light-headed or weightless. Whatever you feel, *you should not feel the existence of any part of your anatomy other than what lies between the crown of your head and the seat.* Being a relaxation as well as sensitization exercise, there is no minimum or maximum time limit.

End the exercise in this way. On your final exhalation, visualize the white vapor above your head dispersing through the air into nothingness. Your next breath should be *consciously taken through the nose.* Swallow your breath, exhale through your mouth, and slowly open your eyes. I stress again the difficulty of this exercise. The beginner may find it hard work at first, but with practice it will become a valuable relaxation tool, brief and effective.

Applying Your Ki

Fundamentals

You may begin applying your ki to yourself and others from the moment you are able to access it. The training exercises should be repeated regularly in order to strengthen and refine your ki as well as to relax and sensitize your body. The procedure used to access ki places the giver in a relaxed state in which she is also susceptible to receiving ki. The average receiver (spouse, friend, parent, child, and so on) does not practice any relaxation technique before receiving ki. The giver, therefore, must always help the receiver relax before applying ki. *Relaxation of the receiver is essential for the effective transmission of ki.*

Relaxation is relative. Some people can hardly ever relax, while others can easily be induced into a state of repose. There is no standard. There are, however, certain guidelines that are useful to follow. *The procedure and guidelines given here should be used at the start of any treatment session using ki. Attempting to leap directly into treatment by bypassing* this procedure usually results in wasted time and effort.

Relaxing the Receiver

The receiver should lie face down with the arms alongside the body. The head should rest on the left cheek, facing right. It is possible to face forward and rest the head on the chin, but this position is difficult to hold. The giver will be on the receiver's left, meaning that the giver's left hand will be at the receiver's head and the right hand will be at the lower back. In Japan, both giver and receiver rest on the floor. The receiver usually lies on a terry-cloth towel. The giver sits with her knees lightly touching the receiver's left arm.

For those who own a massage table, the giver may perform this procedure while standing. The receiver lies on the table, as described, and the giver stands on the left side. Most people will probably find using a bed the most convenient for treatment.

The receiver lies at the edge of the bed. A bed with a firm mattress is best. The giver draws up a backless chair or a low stool to the side of the bed. The procedure may also be performed with the giver sitting at the left edge of the bed.

You are now ready to begin. The receiver should gently close his eyes. The following instructions are for the giver only. *Keep your eyes open throughout the procedure.* With your hands lying comfortably in your lap or hanging loosely at your sides, observe for thirty seconds the breathing of the receiver. It will almost certainly be shallow and rather rapid. Raise your hands above the receiver's spine, palms down. You will look as if you are about to play the piano (figure 14). The left hand should be about *five or six inches* below the neck. The right hand should be placed on the lower spine just above the waistline.

Figure 14

With your hands in midair (and still observing the receiver's breathing) *inhale deeply through the nose and exhale slowly through your palms.* Continue breathing in this way until the end of the procedure.

It is not necessary to be conscious of this breathing. Let it become

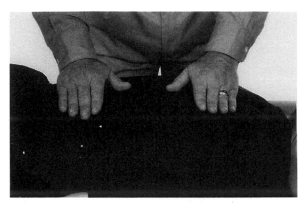

Figure 15

natural. It is more important to be conscious of the receiver's breathing and state of relaxation. Your breathing will be slower than the receiver's. When you observe that the receiver is at the peak of his inhalation (in other words, when the lungs are fully inflated), gently lower your hands to lie on the receiver's spine at the points indicated earlier (figure 15). Feel your hands moving up and down as the back expands and contracts.

Synchronize one of your exhalations to one of the receiver's. *As the receiver begins to exhale, begin also to exhale and send ki from both palms directly into the receiver's spine.* You do not have to synchronize the speed of your exhalation. Exhale as slowly as you like. (Remember that ki is transmitted continuously, not only on the exhalation.)

The beginner may want to repeat internally a positive phrase such as "I am sending ki into his spine," "Ki is coming out of my hands all the time," or "My ki is flowing into his spine." In less than a minute, the receiver's breathing will have slowed and deepened.

Continue transmitting ki to the spine for another *thirty to sixty seconds.* When you feel and observe that the receiver's breathing has slowed as much as it can (it has become steady and rhythmic), synchronize an exhalation with the receiver.

At the top of the receiver's inward breath (when the lungs are fully inflated), begin your exhalation to coincide with that of the receiver. *Consciously send your ki into the receiver's spine.*

When you run out of breath, gently lift your hands off the receiver's back as you inhale. Place them on your lap or at your sides. *The receiver is now ready for treatment.*

With practice, you should be able to induce relaxation in the patient in about a minute. Of course, the longer you continue the procedure, the greater the relaxation will be. This is a calming, relaxing technique, and may be thought of as an addition to the relaxation techniques given later.

Treatments

What follows are techniques for using ki to alleviate many of the shocks our flesh is heir to. It is good to remember that many aches and pains do not require specific recipes for treatment but may be treated directly. If there is a pain in the arm, you may put your finger or hand on the spot and send ki into it. Cuts and scrapes will heal faster if ki is applied directly to them. If the ear aches, cover it with your hand and pour ki in. If your sinuses bother you, put your forefingers alongside your nose at the bridge and apply ki (figure 16).

Do not be afraid to improvise on yourself and others. When you apply ki directly, you may want to repeat internally a positive thought, such as "My ki is easing her pain," "I am sending healing ki directly into the painful spot," or "My ki is working to stop her pain." This sort of positive thinking is beneficial both to the giver and receiver when using ki for health maintenance and healing.

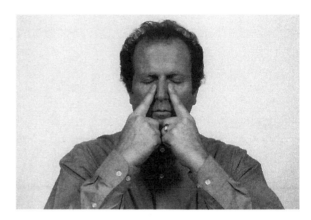

Figure 16

Direct Application of Ki

How you apply ki depends on the size and location of the treated area. Basically, there are three ways of giving ki: through the fingers, through the palms, or through the circular area at the base of the forefinger.

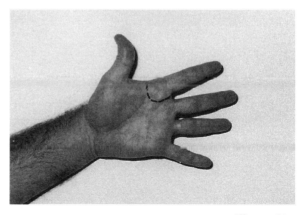

Figure 17

Touch the top of your palm just below the forefinger. You will feel a round bone. This bone is the center of a small circular area (figure 17)

Reference for Locating Points

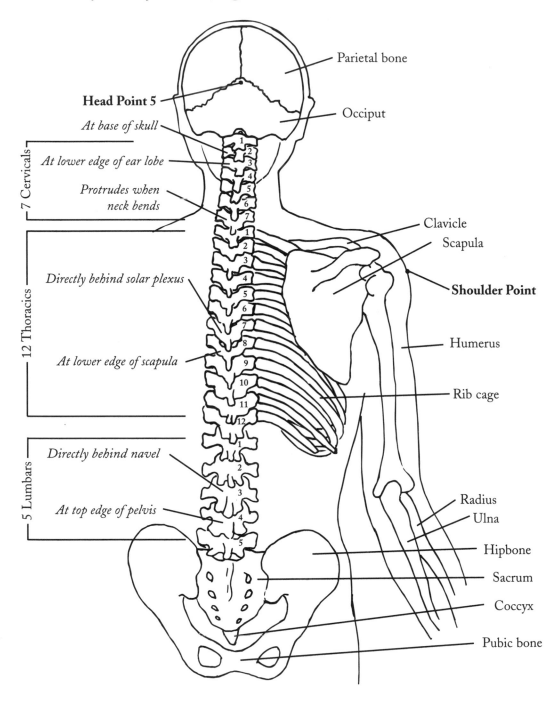

Parietal bone

Head Point 5

Occiput

At base of skull

At lower edge of ear lobe

7 Cervicals

Protrudes when neck bends

Clavicle

Scapula

Shoulder Point

12 Thoracics

Directly behind solar plexus

Humerus

At lower edge of scapula

Rib cage

5 Lumbars

Directly behind navel

Radius

Ulna

At top edge of pelvis

Hipbone

Sacrum

Coccyx

Pubic bone

Head Points 2—Standing behind the receiver, place the forefinger and middle finger of both hands on receiver's temples. Move fingers slightly upward and forward until you encounter a shallow trough, or trench, on both sides. These are the points.

Head Point 5—This is located between the branching arms of the head sutures (the lines formed by the junction of the cranial bones). To find them, trace a line around the head starting from the top of the eyebrow. In the center of the back of the head you will feel a flat spot the size of a small coin. You may also find the spot by tracing gently with your thumbs the line of the sutures. Just below the point where they join is Head Point 5.

Shoulder Point—It is located on both shoulders two to three inches below the top of the shoulder. The shoulder grows rounded, and the point is at the center of the rounded muscle.

Cervical Vertebra 2 (C2)—To work on C2, place your thumbs at the base of the skull on both sides of the spine, about one inch from the spine on each side. You will feel a depression. This becomes easier to feel when the chin is raised.

Cervical Vertebra 7 (C7)—This vertebra protrudes when the neck bends forward. It is the last (southernmost) vertebra to turn when the head turns.

Thoracic Vertebra 1 (T1)—It is the first vertebra that does not turn when the head is turned.

Thoracic Vertebra 5 (T5)—It frequently protrudes.

Thoracic Vertebra 6 (T6)—This one is found directly behind the solar plexus.

Thoracic Vertebra 7 (T7)—It is located in line with the lower edge of the scapula.

Thoracic Vertebra 11 (T11)—It is usually located in the middle of the back where the lowest ribs are attached.

Lumbar Vertebra 3 (L3)—It is found directly behind the navel and corresponds to the waistline.

Lumbar Vertebra 4 (L4)—This vertebra lies in line with the top edge of the pelvis. While standing, place your thumbs at the top of your pelvis and trace a straight line to your spine. You will find L4. This can also be done on a receiver lying facedown.

Sacrum—It runs from below L5 to the top of the crack between the buttocks.

that is highly effective for transmitting ki. For the purpose of this book, I will call this area the "heart" of the hand. It should be used before the other two parts of the hand whenever possible.

Whenever you transfer ki, be sure to begin and end on an exhalation. In most cases, the spot to which you are giving ki will begin to feel warm. It will sometimes feel like the spot is absorbing your ki, almost sucking it up.

In a minute or two, the sensation of warmth will reach its peak, and the area will begin to cool off. In another minute it might even feel slightly cold. This means that the spot has *absorbed all the ki it can.* It is now pointless to transmit more ki. End on an exhalation, and wait an hour before giving more ki.

Ki will frequently remove pain. However, it is better to consider that your ki will first alleviate the pain to some degree and continue working within the spot. Remember that healing with ki is like cooking with microwave—the process goes on at a molecular level after the current has been turned off.

Ki Treatments for Specific Problems

Back Pain

Neck and Upper Back

A stiff neck and/or a tight upper back are often signs of mental stress and tension, even anxiety. To relieve the pain caused by this tension, the brain must first be relaxed.

The receiver sits on a stool so that his feet are firmly planted under him. The arms should be completely relaxed and either lying in the lap or dangling at the sides. The patient's eyes should be shut gently. The giver stands behind the receiver. There are three sutures in the head, their collective shape resembling an upside-down Y. The sutures meet about two inches below the crown in most people. There is a flat spot between where the arms of the Y begin to branch (see Reference for Locating Points, pp. 36 and 37). This spot is the size of a small coin. In most people, it can be covered by the thumb (figure 18) The spot is called Head Point 5.

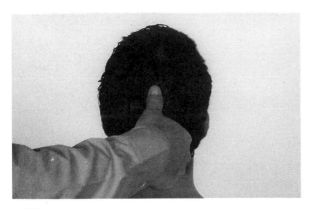

Figure 18

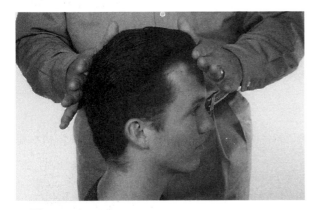

Figure 19

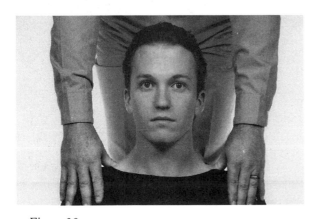

Figure 20

The giver places the heart of the right hand on this point. Walking to the side of the receiver, the giver places the heart of the left hand on the center of the forehead at the hairline. This is called Head Point 1. Begin to put ki into the head through the hearts of both hands (figure 19). The head should resist at first, but after a moment, the hands will feel warm, then hot. Continue giving ki until the warmth subsides or three minutes pass. *Withdraw the hands slowly.* Do not make a sudden movement.

Next, the giver stands behind the receiver. With both thumbs, the giver finds the seventh cervical vertebra (C7), located where the neck meets the body and usually protruding. It is the last vertebra that moves when the neck is turned.

Placing both thumbs on C7, move each thumb along the plane of the shoulder a distance of three thumb spaces. The thumbs should be five to six inches apart. Lean some of your weight into the thumbs (figure 20). You should feel two depressions, or "dimples," beneath your thumbs. Put ki into the body through your thumbs. Imagine the ki going through the body in a straight line.

You should feel upper-back relaxation in most people within two minutes. Extremely tense people will lack depressions and dimples. Put ki into the body through the thumbs for about four minutes.

To end this procedure, put all your weight on the thumbs for the last ten seconds, and *then suddenly and quickly remove your thumbs at the end of your final exhalation.*

Ask the receiver to point out specifically where the worst of the pain and/or stiffness is located. If the area is small enough, use the heart of the hand; if it's large, use the entire palm. Give ki directly to this point for three minutes. *Withdraw the hand slowly.*

Figure 21

Lower Back

Have the receiver lie flat on the floor. Straddle the receiver. Bending from the hips, place your thumbs directly on either side of the third lumbar vertebra (L3). With equal weight on your thumbs, put ki into the body for two minutes (figure 21).

In the final ten seconds, place all your weight on your thumbs and exhale, which will force the receiver also to exhale. At the moment of the giver and receiver's final exhalation, release the thumbs quickly and suddenly. Move your thumbs down to L4 and repeat the procedure.

Sit beside the receiver on the left. Place your right hand over the sacrum so that the heart of the hand is on the center of the sacrum (figure 22).

Put ki into the sacrum for two to three minutes. *Withdraw the hand slowly.* Ask the receiver the specific location of the worst of the pain. Placing your hand over it, give ki as long as the spot feels warm, but no more than five minutes. *Withdraw the hand slowly.*

Figure 22

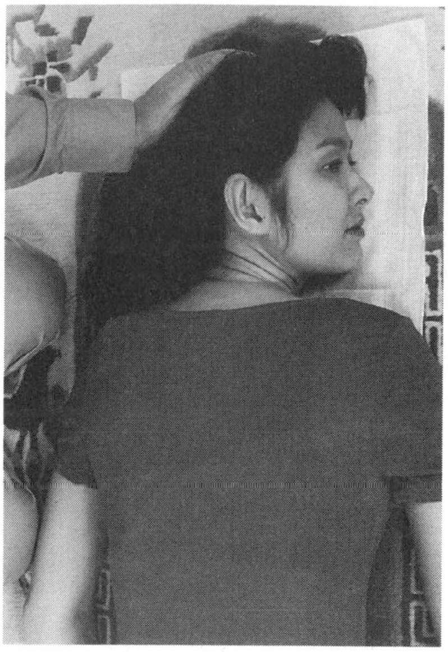

Bed-Wetting

To cure bed-wetting, use the following procedures regularly. The receiver lies facedown. Sit wherever comfortable and place the heart of your hand directly on the crown of the receiver's head (figure 23). Put ki into this point for two to three minutes. *Withdraw your hand slowly.*

In the case of bed-wetting, the first and second lumbar vertebrae are usually too close together. They may even be painful. You can find these vertebrae by locating L3 (see Reference for Locating Points, pp. 36 and 37). Place your hand over them and transmit ki with the entire palm for three to four minutes. *Withdraw your hand slowly.*

If you are sure you have found L1 and L2, straddle the receiver and place your thumbs on either side of L1 (figure 24). Press down, giving ki for two minutes, and then move down to L2 and repeat.

On the final exhalation at each vertebra, press down strongly and release your thumbs quickly and suddenly at the end of the exhalation.

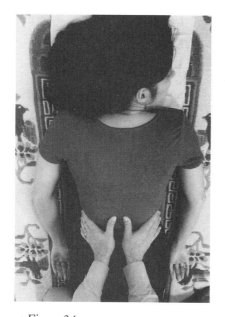

Figure 23

Figure 24

Compulsive Behavior

This procedure, if followed regularly, will curb or even cure unhealthy and addictive habits related to tobacco, liquor, and food. The receiver sits comfortably, eyes closed. The giver sits directly behind. The giver locates Head Point 5. Move the left thumb slowly to the left from the center of the spot until the entire thumb is just outside the spot. Lower the thumb a thumb's breadth (figure 25). Begin transmitting ki into this spot with the left thumb. Place the right hand on the right side of the forehead at the hairline (figure 26).

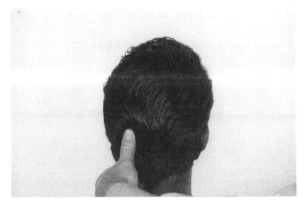

Figure 25

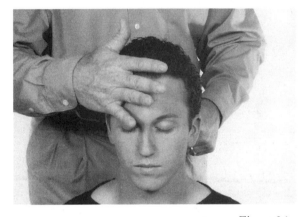

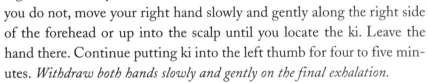

Figure 26

You should feel the ki passing into it from your thumb. If you do not, move your right hand slowly and gently along the right side of the forehead or up into the scalp until you locate the ki. Leave the hand there. Continue putting ki into the left thumb for four to five minutes. *Withdraw both hands slowly and gently on the final exhalation.*

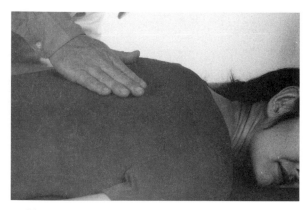

Figure 27

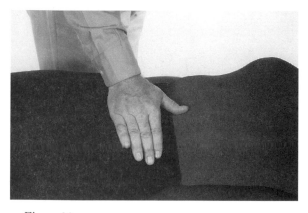

Figure 28

Constipation

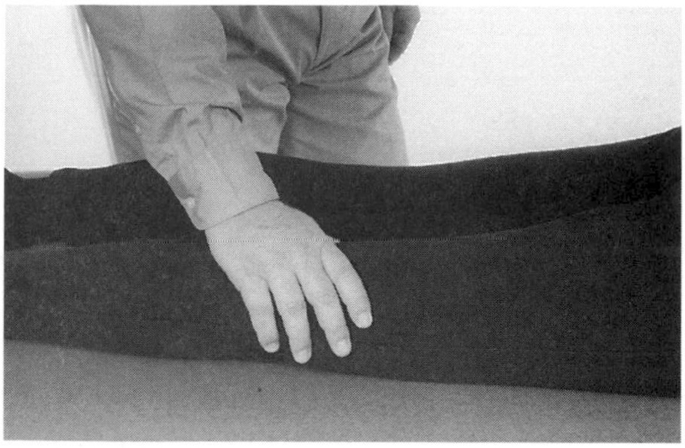

Have the receiver lie facedown on the floor or a massage table. Sitting or standing behind the receiver, place your right hand on the back of the right knee or the left hand over the back of the left knee, whichever feels better for you (figure 27). Send ki into the spot through the heart of your hand for about three minutes. *Withdraw the hand slowly.*

Stand or sit to the left of the receiver. Place your hand over the spine in the center of the back, about two inches below T7 (figure 28). This should correspond to the ninth and tenth thoracic vertebrae (T9 and T10). Put ki into this area with the entire hand for thirty seconds, and then move the hand down slowly a handbreadth and give ki for one minute. Move the hand down again, repeating the procedure until you reach L3, which is at the waistline. Put ki into L3 for one minute. *Withdraw the hand slowly.*

Have the receiver turn over. Sitting or standing on the receiver's right, place your right hand so that the heel of the thumb is on the navel and the rest

Figure 29

of the hand is below and to the left of the navel (figure 29). Put ki into this spot for two minutes. *Withdraw the hand slowly.*

Digestion

For weak or upset stomach, do the following. Look at the back of the receiver's hands between the forefinger and thumb. One should appear larger or more rounded than the other. Grasp this point lightly between your own thumb and forefinger, and put ki in for two to three minutes (figure 30). Withdraw your fingers gently.

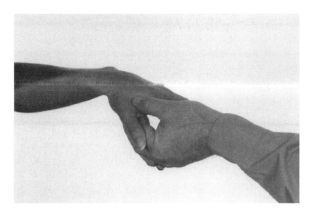

Figure 30

Have the receiver lie on her back. Go to the receiver's feet. Take the heel of the left foot and raise it slightly with your left hand. Grasp the tip of the second toe with your thumb and forefinger (figure 31). The thumb should be on the giver's left side of the toe. Put ki into the toe through your thumb. There is frequently a response, such as a growl from the receiver's stomach. Continue for two to three minutes. Withdraw your fingers gently.

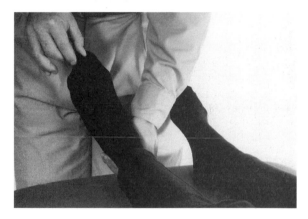

Figure 31

The receiver, still on her back, bends the left leg at the knee, placing the left foot flat on the floor (figure 32). Go to the side of the receiver and send ki with the whole palm to the outside of the left shin from the knee to the ankle.

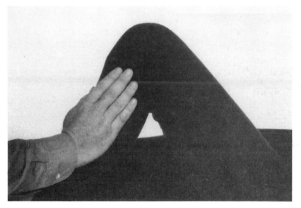

Figure 32

Work your way slowly down the outside of the shin, giving ki for one minute at each spot. Withdraw your hand gently.

Figure 33

Elbow Pain

This method is especially good for treating sports-related pain. The receiver sits or stands. It is important that the receiver allows the arm to become perfectly relaxed. There should not be the least bit of tension in the arm. The giver takes the arm by the wrist and holds the arm out, palm up, toward himself (figure 33). With his free hand, the giver places his thumb and middle finger just below the outside of the elbow on the upper arm (figure 34). There will be two grooves just behind the bone. Put ki into the elbow through the thumb and middle finger for three minutes. *At the end of the final exhalation, release the elbow quickly and sud-*

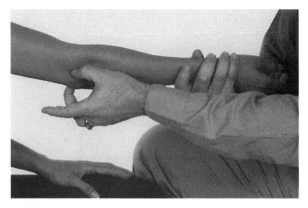

Figure 34

denly but continue holding the wrist. Lower the wrist to the receiver's side.

Eyestrain

The receiver should be lying faceup. The giver sits or stands at his head. Place the thumbs or middle fingers (whichever feels more sensitive and comfortable) in the corners of the receiver's eyes by the side of the bridge of the nose (figure 35). You will feel a hard, tiny bump on either side, something like a grain of sand. Put ki into your fingers and leave them on the points for two minutes. After two minutes, move your fingers very slowly along the top of the eye socket just below the eyebrows, transmitting ki as you go along (figure 36). When you reach the end of the upper eye socket, *withdraw your hand quickly*. Repeat this procedure.

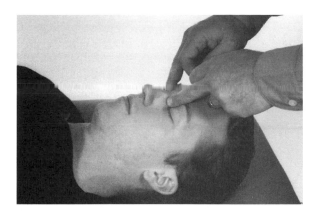

Figure 35

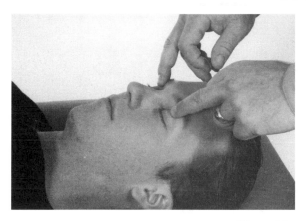

Figure 36

Prolonged eyestrain or fatigue will become apparent in the ears. The receiver sits comfortably. The giver clasps the edge of the outer ear between thumb and forefinger (figure 37). Squeeze gently, following the natural curve of the outer ear. *Do not tug or pull the ear outward*. If the ear is stiff or painful or if the receiver has had blurred vision or seen spots, the giver should gently squeeze the

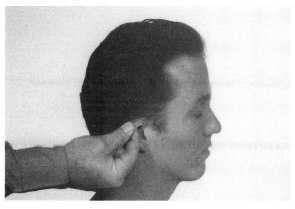

Figure 37

outer ear in its natural direction, giving ki at the same time. Work slowly down from the top of the ear to the lobe. *Release the ear quickly each time*

It is important to squeeze the ear gently the first time. The procedure should be done twice, but more firmly the second time.

Fatigue

Fatigue can arise from a number of sources, including poor diet and poor sleep habits. However, the following three procedures are beneficial for alleviating a sense of fatigue. At the end of these procedures, the receiver may feel tired or sleepy. This feeling is not to be confused with fatigue. This is the feeling of relaxation. A feeling of relaxation accompanied by yawning confirms that this is relaxation; fatigue does not produce yawning.

The receiver sits comfortably in a backless chair with the giver standing behind. The giver takes the forefinger and middle finger of each hand and places them on the temples of the receiver (figure 38). Moving the fingers gently and slowly straight up toward the top of the head, you will encounter a groove or trench in the skull on both sides of the head. Let your fingers rest there. These are called Head Points 2.

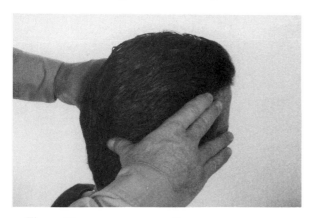

Figure 38

To provide support for these fingers place your thumbs lightly on the back of the skull. Put ki into Head Points 2 with your forefingers and middle fingers for three to five minutes. The bodies of some receivers may begin to move; *this is a natural reaction to ki entering this point.* The movement will end when you stop giving ki. Likewise, some receivers will begin to yawn, sometimes violently. This, too, is a natural reaction. When you have finished giving ki, withdraw your hands gradually.

The receiver then lies facedown. The giver is at the left of the receiver. Place the heart of the right hand over the sacrum of the receiver and give ki for two minutes. *Withdraw the hand quickly at the end of your final exhalation.*

The receiver continues to lie facedown. The giver stands at the feet and places one hand on each Achilles tendon. Put ki into both hands. One side should respond (by getting warm) faster than the other. Remove that hand and concentrate on giving ki to the less sensitive leg.

Continue for two minutes. Should both legs be equally sensitive, give ki to both for two minutes. Withdraw hands slowly.

Hair Loss

This procedure will not restore hair. However, it will greatly slow or even stop the balding process. There is no giver or receiver; one carries out this procedure oneself. Standing, raise your chin as high as it will go. Cross your hands at your throat so that your fingers cover your lower jaw (figure 39). Take a deep breath and exhale loudly through your open mouth, vibrating your vocal cords to produce a sound. As you do this, slowly move your hands straight down your neck putting ki into them (figure 40). Stop when you reach the bottom of the neck. Repeat this procedure six times, making seven in all. *This procedure should be done twice a week.*

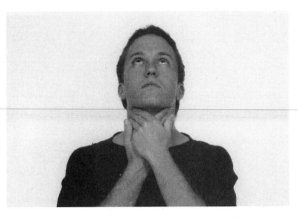

Figure 39

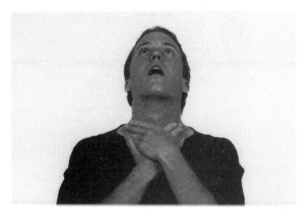

Figure 40

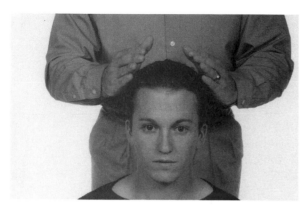

Figure 41

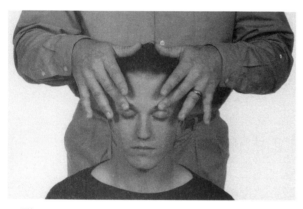

Figure 42

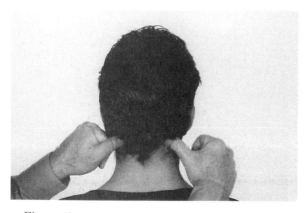

Figure 43

Headache

Ordinary Headache

The receiver should be seated comfortably. The giver stands behind. Cupping the hands, hold them over the receiver's skull (figure 41). Close your eyes. You should feel heat coming from a certain point(s) in the skull. Cover the point(s) with your hand(s) and give ki with the whole hand for two minutes. Withdraw your hand(s) slowly. Still standing behind the receiver, place your middle fingers over the middle of the upper eye sockets (figure 42). Put ki into these points for two minutes. Withdraw your fingers slowly.

Migraine Headache

The receiver is seated comfortably, eyes closed. The giver is behind the receiver, but positioned lower than the receiver. In the case of migraines, the giver puts ki into the second cervical vertebra (C2). At the base of the skull, where it curves into the neck, is a hollow, or depression, on the left and right sides. Your thumbs should find it easily. Put your thumbs into the C2 points (figure 43) and place your remaining fingers comfortably on the side of the receiver's head and face (figure 44).

Put ki into both of your hands. After a minute, you should be able to feel that one side of the neck is tenser than the other. Should you be unable to sense this tension, ask the receiver which side feels more tense. If the receiver is unable to answer, slowly turn the head to the left and then to the right and ask again. One side of the neck will be more tense than the other.

Depending on which side the tension is on, turn the head to either the left or right until there is a balance of tension. This step is very important; be sure to ask the receiver to guide you if your touch is uncertain.

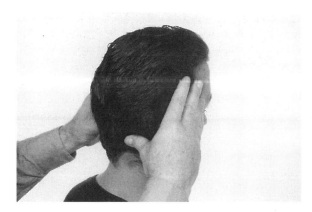

Figure 44

In this position, pull the receiver's head back so that the chin goes up. Your thumbs should sink into the hollows at the base of the skull (figure 45). Ask the receiver to open his eyes wide and look upward as high as possible. Put ki into both of your hands, keeping firm pressure on the thumbs. Continue transmitting ki for one minute. The entire spine, especially the lumbar vertebrae, will tense. After a minute of this tension, *suddenly release the pressure of the thumbs* and let the head return to its normal position. Continue giving ki for thirty seconds and withdraw your hands slowly.

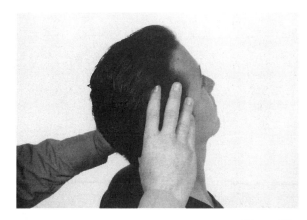

Figure 45

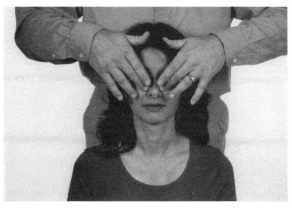

Figure 46

Some women experience migraines in connection with their periods. To alleviate these, use the middle fingers to put ki into the sides of the nose at the bridge for three minutes (figure 46). Hot compresses placed at the sides of the nose at the bridge will also work, though not as well as ki.

Figure 47

Figure 48

Kidneys

This procedure is good not only for kidney failure or dysfunction but also for treating water on the lungs.

The receiver is seated comfortably on a backless chair. The giver sits directly behind. The kidneys are located beneath the left and right scapulae, beginning approximately at the level of the ninth thoracic vertebra. The palms cover the kidneys perfectly.

Put ki into your palms and feel if one or both kidneys respond. Usually one palm will become warm. Keep your palm on the other, *unresponsive* kidney and place your free hand on the other side of the body just below the rib cage (figure 47).

Put ki into the free hand for two minutes. You should feel the hand on the kidney become warm. Move the free hand down the receiver's side a handbreadth (figure 48).

Put ki into both hands for two minutes. Move the free hand down one more handbreadth and put ki into both hands for two minutes. Withdraw both hands slowly.

In the event that the left and right kidneys seem balanced at the beginning, simply put ki directly into them with both palms for five minutes.

Next, the receiver lies facedown. The giver is positioned at the receiver's feet. Taking the receiver's right foot in your right hand, place your thumb on a point one to two inches below the fourth toe (figure 49). This point will feel slightly squishy. Place your left hand under your right hand and your left thumb on top of your right thumb. Put ki into your thumbs. Consciously direct your ki to the receiver's kidneys.

Continue for three minutes, and then *withdraw your thumbs suddenly at the end of your final exhalation.* This procedure should be carried out daily. For minor kidney problems, have the receiver lie facedown and put ki directly into T11 for five minutes a day.

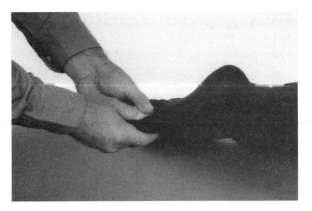

Figure 49

Knee Pain

The receiver lies faceup and bends the painful knee until the foot is flat upon the floor. The giver sits at the side of the receiver and sandwiches the knee with both hands (figure 50). Put ki into the knee with both hands for three minutes, withdrawing the hands slowly at the end. Go to the foot of the patient. Take the heel of the bent leg in your hand and *firmly and quickly* pull the leg out straight (figure 51). The mo-ment the leg is straight, place your free hand firmly on the kneecap and transmit ki with the whole hand for two minutes. Withdraw your hand slowly.

Figure 50

Figure 51

Menstrual Problems

This procedure is good for regulating periods and reducing cramping and other pain. I have heard that it also has a positive effect in alleviating the symptoms of premenstrual syndrome. There are two ovaries, but only one is active each month. The ovaries work in alternation, one spelling the other. There are two ways of ascertaining which ovary is working that month. (Once you ascertain which is working in a particular month, it is simple to keep track of whose turn it is.)

The first way is through assessing breast soreness. One breast will usually be more tender or painful than the other before menses. That breast corresponds to the working ovary. A painful left breast means the left ovary is at work. In the event that it is difficult to judge which is more tender or painful, the woman should lie on her back, her arms at her sides. The giver, using the fore-, middle, and ring fingers, puts gentle pressure along the base of the breast where it meets the side of the body by the arm. There should be a tender spot.

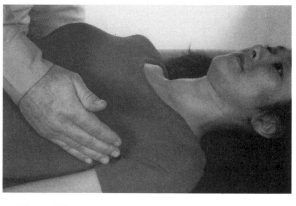

Figure 52

This spot is easy to find by using ki, for it will be warm. The giver cups the hand and places the palm slightly above the base of the breast and seeks a heat-producing point (figure 52). When that point is found, put ki into that point with the middle finger until it ceases to be tender. The breast with the tender point will correspond to the working ovary. Putting ki into the tender spot of the breast should be done every month one week before the (likely) onset of menses.

The other way to locate the working ovary is by seeing or feeling the ovaries. The ovaries are usually located about three inches above the pubic bone and to the sides. When the woman lies on her back, there should be two very slight mounds that may be seen from the side. One of the mounds will be quivering slightly, the other will be inert. The quivering side is the working ovary. In form and in feel the area above the ovaries is similar to marshmallows.

It is also possible to feel the working ovary by means of ki. Having visually located the ovaries (the woman herself can locate her ovaries by means of touch while lying on her back), the giver places the fore-, middle, and ring fingers of the left hand on the right ovary and those of the right hand on the left ovary (figure 53). Send ki into both ovaries. One will respond by becoming warm, and the other will remain unresponsive. The unresponsive ovary is resting.

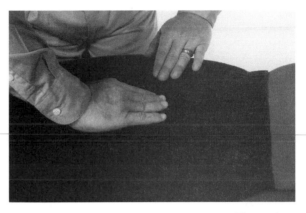

Figure 53

The day after the menstrual blood turns brown is the time to begin putting ki into the *resting ovary*. This should be done for three consecutive days. Each day will become easier as the resting ovary revs up and the working ovary closes down. There is no standardized length of time for giving ki to a resting ovary; it depends on the susceptibility of the individual. Keep sending ki until you feel the ovary begin to quiver. The woman receiving the ki should feel the onset of movement.

A woman may do her own ovarian procedure. Lying on her back, she sends ki through the resting ovary by means of her breath. As she lies on her back, she inhales through her spine and exhales out through the resting ovary, consciously aiming the breath upward at the ceiling. She should place her hands above, but not touching her ovaries to feel for ki passing through a single ovary. This is done simply to ascertain that ki is flowing through the proper ovary. Month by month, the ovaries will respond more strongly to the ki, which may be felt as high as eight inches above the body.

If this breathing technique is difficult, the woman can follow a different procedure. Place the middle finger directly over the resting ovary and have the ovary suck ki out of the finger. In other words, rather than send ki into the ovary through the finger, consciously inhale through the ovary and concentrate on sucking the ki out of the finger with each breath. The exhaled breath goes out from the nose.

Ki Treatments for Specific Problems

Neck Ache

In addition to the procedures described under Headache (p. 50), the following method is extremely effective for chronic neck ache or stiffness. The receiver lies faceup. The giver sits or stands at the receiver's right. The left hand goes under the neck so that the fore-, middle, and ring fingers are holding the neck. Turn the neck *slowly* to the left and right, asking which position feels more comfortable. Turn the head to the comfortable side. At the same time, put the heart of the right hand over the solar plexus (figure 54). Send ki into the neck and solar plexus at the same time for three to four minutes. Turn the neck back to center, and as you do, *withdraw both hands slowly*.

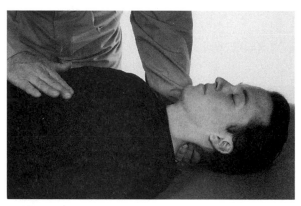

Figure 54

For the next exercise, the receiver sits comfortably. The giver sits or stands behind. Have the receiver turn her head slowly to the left, then the right. As the head turns, you will see a muscle appear, which runs from the top to the bottom of the neck. Cupping your hand, place it over the muscle on the stiff side of the neck and have the receiver return her head to center. Put ki into the muscle with your entire hand for three to four minutes. *Withdraw your hand slowly at the end of your final exhalation.*

Respiratory Problems

The fourth thoracic vertebra (T4) frequently protrudes when there is respiratory weakness. The same may also be true for T5. Begin by putting ki directly into T4 and T5. The receiver may be sitting or lying facedown (figure 55). Next, send ki into the elbow as you would for elbow pain. Then clasp the elbow at top and bottom with both hands and transmit ki for two minutes (figure 56). Finally, put ki into Head Point 5.

Figure 55

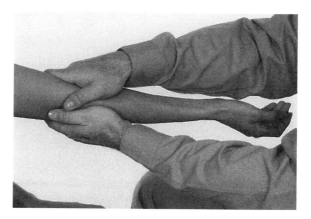

Figure 56

Have the receiver lie facedown. One of the buttocks will be out of alignment. You may check this by placing the edge of your hands at the edge of the buttocks (figure 57). One buttock will be lower than the other, indicating poor pelvic alignment. Put your thumb in the center of the back of the upper thigh corresponding to the unaligned buttock (figure 58). Press down firmly. Put ki into the thumb for thirty seconds and then move it down the thigh an inch; transmit ki for another thirty seconds. You should move down the entire thigh from the base of the but-

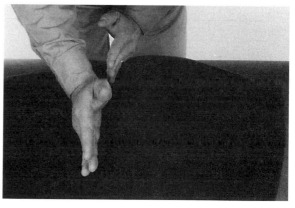

Figure 57

tock to the top of the back of the knee (figure 59). *Release your thumb suddenly each time before you move farther down the thigh.*

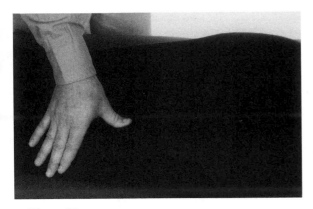

Figure 58

The receiver moves to a sitting position. There are two prominent bones at the base of the neck alongside the hollow of the throat. Place your middle fingers on them (figure 60). One will be higher than the other. Put ki into the *lower* one for three minutes. *Withdraw your fingers quickly.*

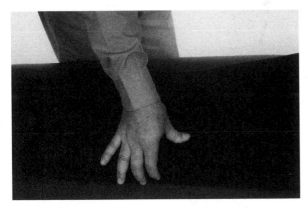

Figure 59

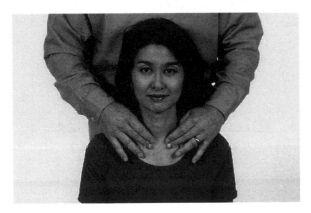

Figure 60

Shoulder Pain and Stiffness

The receiver may sit or stand, the giver positioned behind. The receiver raises the arm with the stiff shoulder. It will stick or feel sore at a certain angle. At this point, the receiver should tense the arm and shoulder. The giver places her hand over the sore point (or over the upper scapula, if the point is not precise—figure 61) and gives ki for one to two minutes. At the conclusion, the receiver and giver must work in concert. They should both exhale together. At the end of the exhalation, when the breath is exhausted, the giver quickly removes her hand, and the receiver relaxes the arm and lets it drop to the side.

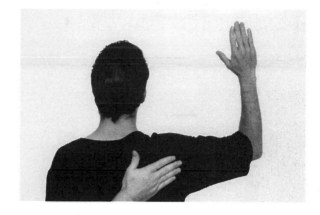

Figure 61

Next, the receiver sits comfortably with eyes closed. The giver sits perpendicular to the receiver's stiff/sore shoulder. Using whichever thumb feels more comfortable, the giver places it on the Shoulder Point. This is located two to three inches below the top of the shoulder, in the center of the rounded muscle. Place the free hand on top of the shoulder for support (figure 62). Press gently but firmly with the thumb and put ki into the Shoulder Point

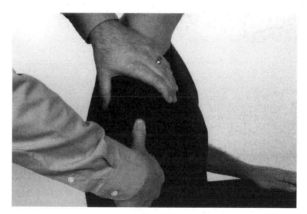

Figure 62

for three minutes. *Withdraw the thumb quickly and suddenly at the end of the final exhalation.*

The receiver continues sitting, and the giver sits behind the receiver. Working on the right shoulder, place your right hand under the receiver's armpit so that the right thumb is on the *back* of the shoulder and the rest of the hand rests on the *chest.*

Place the left hand over the clavicle so that the left thumb meets the

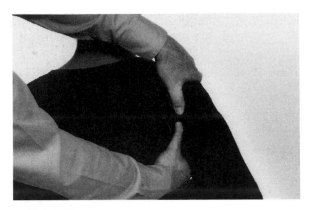

Figure 63

right thumb (figure 63). (When working on the left shoulder, the hands are reversed.) The thumbs should form a single line along where the shoulder is attached to the body. Pressing gently but firmly with the thumbs, transmit ki into the shoulder for four to five minutes. *Release the thumb pressure quickly and suddenly on your last exhalation.*

Sleep Disorders

The following procedures, performed regularly in conjunction with total body relaxation, will induce deep, satisfying sleep.

Sleep disorders generally manifest themselves in one of two (or both) places. The first is at the base of the skull, corresponding to C2. If you are able to pinch and hold the skin at this point, it indicates a sleep disorder. The second is a tender spot beneath the clavicle where the *right* shoulder meets the body. There is a natural hollow there, which becomes tender to the touch under the influence of a sleep disorder.

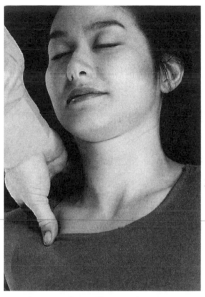

Figure 64

To locate the sleep point beneath the clavicle, have the receiver lie faceup. Sitting behind the receiver *or* on the receiver's right side, feel for the hollow with your right thumb. Press gently but firmly on the spot (figure 64). If it is tender, put ki into it with your thumb for two minutes. *Withdraw the thumb quickly.*

Have the receiver roll over and lie facedown. Sitting at the left, place your right palm directly over the center of the sacrum and give ki with your entire hand for two minutes. *Withdraw the hand gently.* Next, the receiver sits, eyes closed. Put ki into the head at Head Points 5 and 1, as explained under Neck and Upper Back. Finally, transmit ki into the right palm with your right thumb, as explained under Brain Tension (p. 62).

Tension

Brain

To relax the brain, use Head Points 5 and 1, as explained under Neck and Upper Back. In addition, use the following procedure. The receiver sits comfortably, and the giver sits or stands at the receiver's left. Place the right hand at the right base of the skull and the left hand at the hairline on the left of the forehead (figure 65). The hands should be positioned so that the ki from the right hand will go upward in a diagonal line into the left hand. Transmit ki from the *right hand only* for four minutes. You should feel the ki in your left hand and be able to monitor its strength. *Withdraw your hands very slowly, continuing to give ki until your hands are three inches from the head.*

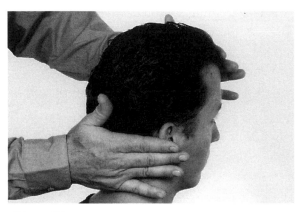

Figure 65

The receiver continues sitting comfortably with eyes closed, and the giver sits or kneels at his feet. Take the receiver's right hand in your right hand. With your left hand, support the arm at the elbow. Place your thumb in the center of the receiver's palm and send ki in. Continue transmitting ki for one minute. With your right hand, push the receiver's arm gently toward her. This will have the effect of putting her slightly off balance. In this position continue sending in ki for one more minute. You should feel a tiny, hard lump, like a bead, appear in the center of the palm under your thumb. *Withdraw your hand gently and lower the receiver's arm.*

Total Body

The receiver lies faceup, hands at sides and eyes closed. The giver sits or stands at the receiver's right, facing in the direction of the receiver's head. Run the right hand slowly over, *but not touching*, the left side of the body from the rib cage to the hip bone (figure 66). Feel for a warm or

hot spot on the body. Should
you find none, move your hand a
handbreadth in toward the center of the body and back again,
north to south. If you fail to find
a warm/hot spot, move right
another handbreadth and try
again. There is sure to be such a
spot somewhere between the rib
cage and the pelvis.

Figure 66

When you locate the spot,
place the heart of your right hand on it. Close your eyes. Put ki into the
spot until your hand and the spot are evenly warm/hot. Move your hand
an inch upward, taking the spot with you. Put ki into the spot until an
equilibrium of warmth between the receiver and giver is reached again.
Then move the warm spot upward another inch and repeat the procedure. Little by little, you will bring the warm/hot spot up toward the
receiver's solar plexus.

The goal of this procedure is to move the warm/hot spot to the center of the receiver's solar plexus. This usually takes about five to six minutes. When your hand is covering the solar plexus, *stop giving ki with the
heart of the hand and begin giving ki with the entire hand.* After a while it
will not be necessary to put ki in consciously. The receiver will suck it
out of your hand. A warmth will spread through the receiver's body,
radiating out from the solar plexus. (Many people fall asleep at this
point). *Remove your hand very slowly and continue to sit or stand by the side
of the receiver.* Do not make any sudden movement or motion likely to
jar the receiver, who will open his eyes naturally when it is comfortable
to do so.

Toothache

The teeth become very sensitive from autumn to early winter. If at all possible, it is best to avoid having dental work from October through January.

The following procedures should be followed in the case of toothache or from pain following dental work.

The receiver sits comfortably, eyes closed. The giver sits facing the receiver at the side corresponding to the painful side of the mouth. If the right side hurts, sit on the right. Grasp the arm gently beneath the elbow and hold the arm out straight. Place your thumb just below the elbow joint and put ki into it for two minutes. *Release the thumb pressure quickly.* Move your thumb into the elbow joint and transmit ki for two minutes (figure 67). Then move your thumb up to just above the elbow joint and repeat the procedure.

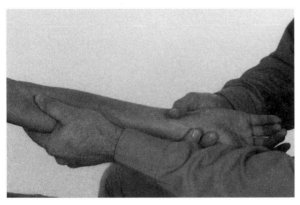

Figure 67

Next, place your forefinger and middle finger on the face over the affected area and give ki for three to four minutes. *Remove your fingers gradually.*

PART II

THE KI OF
MRS. MATSUURA

Chapter 1

Mrs. Matsuura's practice was located in Odawara, about an hour by express train from downtown Tokyo. The building was set atop a hill overlooking a small cemetery and gave an expansive view of the town and the Pacific Ocean, which always shimmered a dull silver, whatever the weather. Outside the building was a garden. Green shoots were pushing their way through the frigid, dry soil to greet the oncoming spring. A plum tree was swollen with tight buds that promised to burst open in a week if only the warm spell continued. Within, the building was spacious, bright, and airy, filled with people in varying stages of pain and misery. They, too, had come to see the old woman as a last resort, all traditional avenues of healing having proved futile. A Mozart violin concerto was playing over loudspeakers. The atmosphere was subdued but tinged with hope and extravagant expectation.

There was no waiting room, just a large open area with a tatami-covered floor. People sat, stood, lounged, and sprawled where they liked as they waited their turns. About half the patients appeared to have back ailments. The others displayed a variety of complaints. There were young women who had come to be cured of infertility. Other patients were elderly and wanted to have their bodies reshaped and restructured following the removal of an organ, most from cancer surgery. A number of infants, the children of X-ray technicians, had congenital defects. Several patients were perfectly healthy and were there only to have their bodies fine-tuned.

Kayoko Matsuura was one of many practitioners of a fairly recent healing and health maintenance technique based on ki energy. I had never heard of the organization and, until I received treatment, confused it with a form of Japanese chiropractic. I was, therefore, a bit chary at first, but Okamoto assured me that the two techniques had nothing in common. More than that he could not say. He was not in the least able to enlighten me as to what Mrs. Matsuura actually did, but he stressed again and again that it worked. Nor was he interested in the physiological principles behind the healing. He was interested only in results, which had been so beneficial that he was content to entrust his body to Mrs. Matsuura without question. He advised me to do likewise.

Mrs. Matsuura worked in the far corner of the room behind a folding screen. She made little noise. She spoke in an undertone, and from time to time I could hear her through the background music, sipping noisily from a glass. A tall handsome man of about thirty, named Furukawa, was her apprentice. It was he who brought people behind the screen when their turns came, it was he who helped her manipulate some of the larger patients, and it was he who changed the classical records. This last seemed to be the most demanding of his duties, for Mrs. Matsuura liked working to music. Furukawa performed this last duty with a grace and dignity that would not have been out of place at an altar. Indeed, the reverence that was paid to the area behind the screen and to the needs and comfort of Mrs. Matsuura suggested a sacerdotal presence.

We waited two hours to be seen. It was a pleasant wait, eased by the novelty of the surroundings. I was instructed to stand upon a machine called a weight distribution measuring device (the wording is not clumsy in Japanese). The machine measured the distribution of my body weight on three points of the sole of each foot, the left ball, the right ball, and the heel. I was told to make simple movements—raising my hands over my head, twisting right and left, squatting, bowing from the waist—and the machine printed out the weight distribution for each movement.

Each movement, I later found out, was related to a certain vertebra, and by reading the printout, the practitioner could know at a glance which vertebrae were out of alignment and to what degree. The procedure was a system for diagnosing not only the body's present condition but also the body's ideal condition. Mrs. Matsuura would later confirm the results with her hands.

Sitting quietly and viewing the spacious ocean, surrounded by people whose sufferings were at least equal to mine, produced a warm, reassuring feeling. I had a vaguely benevolent impulse to wish them all a speedy cure, while not really caring how their treatments turned out. For during the long waiting period I had become possessed by the conviction that this as yet unseen woman would heal me. As long as I recover, that's all that matters, I thought with sublime equanimity. At the time the thought struck me as neither hard-hearted nor selfish. It was an undeniable truth.

When at last my turn came and I was face to face with my eventual savior, it took a powerful act of will to cling to my conviction. She was older than I had imagined. I had expected someone in her early sixties, and this woman appeared ten years older. She was pitifully small, with the baby-bird-like body seen in rural women of her undernourished generation. She was at least an inch under five feet and could not have weighed more than eighty pounds. Her face was thin and bony, without any fleshy padding. The skin clung tightly to her fine cheekbones but slackened somewhat around the eyes, giving them an unusually large and intense appearance. But what almost sent me running for the door was her hair. It was cropped close to the skull and dyed ghastly colors. Either she was the harbinger of punk in Odawara or she conditioned her hair with dyes the way some people season stews, using everything in the pantry. My doubts of her competence were assuaged by a careful look at her eyes and fingers. Her large eyes flashed intelligently as she scanned my printout with a rare economy of motion. Her fingers were long, thin, and agile. Her posture was superb. She sat on the tatami in the classical Japanese manner, on her knees, her back perfectly straight, and her hands resting lightly on her lap.

She instructed me to remove all my clothes but my long underwear and undershirt and to put on the clean pair of socks that I had brought on the advice of Okamoto. I lay facedown on the narrow felt mat spread over the tatami. She asked me one or two trivial questions, more to break the ice than to get information. She was very difficult to understand. She spoke softly and quickly, hardly using her mouth to form words, which she puffed out with a whish-whishing sound.

I had written my ailment as precisely as possible on a sheet of paper: herniated disc of the third lumbar vertebra, resulting in sciatica of the left leg. She read this with my printout. She called Furukawa to look at me with her and then ran her fingers lightly over my spinal cord from the neck to the coccyx. Her fingers through the cotton shirt were warm, almost hot. She had me roll over and then ran her fingers over my chest and abdomen, pausing for about ten seconds at my solar plexus. Then she stood up, walked to my feet, and scanned me from that angle. She mumbled a few observations to Furukawa, pointing energetically at my body as she guided him around it. She sat down beside me again, had me roll over onto my belly, and laid her hands on the small of my back.

She said, "I am so pleased to meet you. I meet so few people with a body as wonderful as yours. You're in excellent health. Your organs are all functioning perfectly, your skin is clear, your muscles are firm but resilient. You should consider yourself a lucky man. It's really a pleasure to touch you. There's just one little thing wrong, but we'll soon clear it up. This is going to be very easy." Her Japanese was slightly old-fashioned, but very polite and nostalgically feminine. She turned to Furukawa. "Hold his hand and monitor his responses. Let's get to work."

I was close to certain she was mad. If not mad, then she was most assuredly gibbering in premature senility. After all, doctors, with varying degrees of drama, tell one how bad one's body is. At best, a physician will say there is nothing wrong with one. Never had I had my body complimented by anyone in the healing profession. The fact that one is there to be "healed" bespeaks a breakdown in the healthy functioning of the organism. "But I'm in terrible pain," I said in a voice that demanded her to look again and consider.

She was unperturbed. "Of course you're in terrible pain. That's because you have a healthy body. If you weren't in pain, there'd be something wrong with you. Imagine having a pinched nerve and not being in terrible pain."

She rose and straddled me. Placing her thumbs on either side of my third lumbar vertebra, she pressed down, telling me to breathe out as hard as I could as she pressed. She then repeated the procedure to my fourth and fifth lumbars. Next she had me roll over. She held my left foot by the heel, raised it six inches off the floor, and then smacked the heel twice with the heel of her palm. Finally, she told me to bend my knees until my heels were close to my behind and arch myself upward so that my feet and head were supporting my weight. As I did this, she had me exhale as powerfully as I could. The instant my breath was about to expire and my body was beginning to tremble from the strain, she pulled my legs straight out from under me, and I came down with a pleasant thump.

She looked at Furukawa, who was lightly holding my hand. He smiled with satisfaction. Another success, he seemed to say. She cradled my neck in her hands, her warm fingers pulsing on the back of my neck. She felt what she called the pulse in the palm of my right hand, felt the area of my solar plexus for a short time, and then had me roll over so that she could trip down the length of my spine with her hands.

"You're all better," she said. "Don't bathe or have liquor for twenty-four hours. You'll be better in the morning." The treatment had taken twenty-five minutes, and I felt no different.

I watched as she worked on Okamoto, but could divine no logical or systematic method of treatment. Indeed, it seemed as intuitive and unknowable as Okamoto had implied.

Furukawa saw me to the door and shuffled sheepishly while I put on my shoes. "Sensei [a term of respect applied to professional people] tends to be a little overly optimistic. As this is your first experience with her, you may interpret her wrongly. You may be better in the morning, but then you may not."

"Am I or am I not better?" I asked peevishly.

"You're physically perfect," he said with unflappable courtesy and retired to his niche behind the screen. "Physically perfect"—I wasn't sure what that meant, but I liked the sound.

On the train ride back to Tokyo I became feverish and broke out in a heavy sweat. I was irresistibly sleepy. I slept and sweated for the length of the trip. Okamoto was not sure if this had anything to do with Mrs. Matsuura's treatment. I was probably catching a cold. The fever died away as abruptly as it had begun, and I gleefully suspected Mrs. Matsuura's influence. The reaction indicated a potency of treatment.

We phoned Patrick from the train station and went out to have a celebratory dinner that evening. The release of two young men from the confines of pain. Here's to health. Cheers. I was feeling jaunty and more pain free than usual. I thanked Okamoto, thanked Patrick, thanked my lucky stars, and then rose to leave. With my change of posture, I experienced a shooting pain of needlelike sharpness throughout my body. The piercing intensity of the sensation made me scream out and carried me to the edge of unconsciousness. I felt limp and dreamy. Okamoto and Patrick leaped up, and each grabbed an arm to support me. The pain lasted a full minute. I thought, "If the nerve weren't pinched, I wouldn't have this pain." I told Okamoto that the old woman had done me as little good as the others. He shook his head and advised me to wait until morning before I wrote her off.

It was difficult not to take a dim view of her, the strange occurrences in my body notwithstanding. I had understood what every other physician and practitioner had done to me. That their treatments had been ineffective was the fault of the technique and not of the practitioner. Not a single person who had seen me had failed to be suitably impressed by the gravity of my condition; some had even put me off with their exaggerated concern. Mrs. Matsuura had been so brief and gentle, so blithely confident in her treatment that I was doubtful that she had understood the profundity of my ailment and thought that she had been preying upon my wishful gullibility to give me a momentary psychological boost.

As I then understood the common sense of healing, the pain should cease the moment the nerve was released. The orthopedic surgeon who would have performed the laminectomy had all but guaranteed me instant freedom from pain following the operation. The conviction that Mrs. Matsuura was my last best hope was rapidly leaving me. I felt inclined to worry again.

The next morning I was paralyzed from the neck down. I opened my eyes and tried to raise my hand, but could feel nothing. My body felt severed from my head. I was in no pain. I panicked and grew feverish. I could turn my head from side to side and use my facial muscles, but the rest of me felt as if it were anesthetized. Had I been less frightened, I would have cried from the irony of my situation: the prospect of incurable pain had forced me to take a reckless leap from the known to the unknown. I seemed to have landed in the clutches of an incompetent quack whose ministrations left me praying for a return of my old, familiar ailment.

The phone was lying only inches from my fingertips. I forced myself to concentrate on reaching it, and the fingers slowly came to life. I got the receiver to my ear and dialed Mrs. Matsuura's number. I swore to change to a push-button phone should I ever regain the power of movement. Flat on my back, with only my mouth moving, I engaged her in the following memorable conversation.

MF (almost choked by panic and anger): I'm paralyzed from the neck down! What have you done to me?! You said I'd be better this morning, and now I'm totally paralyzed!
KM (elated): Totally paralyzed? Why, that's wonderful! Congratulations! You're very lucky.
MF (becoming savage): To hell with your luck! Get me out of this mess!
KM: Thank you for phoning. It was nice of you to take the trouble to inform me of your progress. Call me back if there's a change in your condition.
MF: The next change is likely to be death.
KM: Pull yourself together! Don't you realize this means you're better? You've had a reaction. I told you that you have a wonderful body, very receptive and sensitive.
MF: Will you stop complimenting my body and give me some advice?
KM: You'll regain movement in about two hours.
MF: Then what?
KM: That's it. I'm telling you that you're all better. Look, I'm busy. Come back and see me tomorrow if you're so worried.

Within two hours I had regained feeling and was moving about easily. The pain had shifted from my calf and was jumping around between the toes and the hip, alighting and then immediately taking off like a jittery thing. The old woman had obviously worked some sort of powerful medicine on me, but still I mistrusted and had black thoughts about her all day.

On Thursday the building was empty. Furukawa sat in the small kitchen reading, looking up to nod at me in greeting but not bothering to inquire how I was getting on. The stereo was unattended. Mrs. Matsuura was writhing on her back like an overturned snake, rolling and twisting,

twisting and rolling. I was not heartened. She lacked the dignified and studied aplomb I had come to expect from medical practitioners. I tapped the tip of my crutch on the tatami to announce my presence. She signaled to me to wait a moment.

"Got a violent itch?" I asked.

"I'm glad you've come," she whished from the floor, "I was afraid I'd have nothing to do today."

"What was that all about?" I asked when she had finished her writhing and was sitting still.

"Just doing my exercise. Don't you ever see animals stretching and rolling on their backs? Straightens the spinal cord. You ought to try it."

She did not measure my weight distribution. I lay down fully clothed on my belly, describing as graphically and ruefully as I could the events that had passed since my treatment.

She sympathized with my living arrangements rather than with my fear. "You'd have been all right if you had a wife or a girlfriend. I prefer to see people as couples. It's very important to have the healthy partner understand exactly what the ill partner is suffering and give useful support and encouragement. You would have found yesterday much easier to take if you'd had a sympathetic partner."

She ran her fingers lightly over my spinal cord and had me turn over. She held my head in her hands and squeezed my neck. She felt my solar plexus and spent a minute lingering over points on my abdomen.

"You have trouble urinating," she announced. "You haven't had a good pee in months. It doesn't gush out like it should." She traced a line with her forefinger down the inside of my right thigh, eliciting intense pain.

"Yes, your urinary tract needs fixing," she said matter-of-factly, pulled my right leg straight out and to my right as far as it would go, and then placed her palm on the inside of the thigh. She began making small talk. Food production both fascinated and worried her. She had grave doubts that it was in the nature of things to have strawberries year round. What would be the effect on an organism that changed with the seasons of eating foods that did not? Are hothouse fruits and vegetables as nutritious as those grown outdoors, she wondered aloud. As she spoke, her palm grew warm, then hot. My leg began to tingle. She carried on talking about food prices, leaving off my leg to feel my neck from time to time. She gently replaced my leg in its original position and traced the same line as before. There was no pain.

"You'll enjoy urinating again," she said.

She ran both hands over the length of my body, then sat beside me and held my hand. Her thumb was on the base of my right thumb. Her touch was assured and powerful. Her thumb grew warm; she pressed harder, and I felt a dull ache throughout my body. "Just bear it," she said, and in a minute the pain began diminishing sensibly until it vanished. When she was satisfied, she did the same to the heel and toes of my left foot.

"You're in great shape," she said and bowed to me on her knees, formally concluding the session. "Stand up and let me have a look at you." She was pleased with what she saw. She smiled a sweet, broad smile. "Come back in a month for another treatment," she said and made to leave the room.

"What should I do until then?" I was bewildered by her (to me) cavalier attitude.

"Have fun. Go skiing."

"How can I ski when my leg is still in such pain?"

"Skiing will take your mind off the pain, especially if you're a bad skier. You'll have to concentrate on your form."

"Won't that upset the treatment?"

"Not at all. You're all better. I keep telling you that."

"That's what I'd like to talk to you about," I said and poured out the list of grievances I had been compiling for two days.

"The orthopedic surgeon told me that the moment my nerve was freed I would be out of pain. He promised me instant relief with surgery. You tell me I'm fine, but I hurt worse than ever," I concluded, implying that she had failed to live up to the surgeon's promise.

She was taken aback. "He said that? You must have misunderstood How could he say such a thing? And for you to believe him . . . an intelligent man like you!"

"I don't see how my intelligence has led me astray," I countered. "If the nerve's pinched, it hurts; if it's free, it doesn't."

"The two of you certainly have a strange idea of the human body," she said, showing concern for the first time since I had met her. My physical condition had not fazed her, but my outlook was distressing. She slapped her high, lined forehead and muttered to herself; then she called to Furukawa to bring her guitar.

"Let me show you something." She strummed random notes. She

then depressed one of the strings with her thumb and told me to pluck it. It did not resonate.

"That was your nerve. Now watch what happens when it's suddenly released." She took her thumb from the string, which twanged and vibrated wildly.

"Your nerve was like that string, only a living string straining to get free. It was depressed for at least eighteen months. What do you think it's doing now that nothing is holding it down? It's vibrating, pulsing, returning to life and vigor. It's probably a little hard for it to believe it's free again. Our bodies, like ourselves, quickly fall into a routine. If you thought you were in pain while the nerve was pinched, you'll be in agony now that it's free."

I was dismayed. She made sense, but then so had the physicians.

"What do I do for the pain?" I asked.

"Do? Go on living. It will go away. Whatever you do, don't take medication. It will only slow the healing process and undo my work. I'll know if you've been taking medicine and will refuse to treat you."

"How long until it goes away?"

She shrugged. "Every body is different. You have a remarkably sensitive body. Your reaction was so immediate and pronounced that you should be over the pain within a year."

I was as angry as a child who, faced with an unpleasant truth, preferred a congenial deception.

"Barring an accident, you'll have another fifty years of healthy life. What's so terrible about a year? Besides, what choice do you have?"

That was her exit line, and a rather neat one I thought. It left no room for a comeback.

I had always been a healthy, cheerful person. The few encounters I had had with physicians had been brief, and relief had been as instantaneous as they had promised. One took aspirin for headaches until something "faster and more effective" came along, and then one took that. There was a spiraling escalation in speed of relief for all over-the-counter drugs bought to quell the thousand natural aches and pains of the flesh. Speed is the most potent allure of all our medical panaceas. It is our culture's ultimate desideratum. With so many psychic and emotional tugs and strains, we feel we have the right to be excused from extended bodily pain. And when a cure is not readily available, are we not told that doctors and scientists are racing to find one? All we need do is urge them on with financial encouragement for them to reach the finish line before our pain and illness overcome us. I believed in speed, worshiped speed, and yearned for a speedy return to health as I understood it. I cringed at the thought of walking the road of heresy along which the body mended itself in its own good time.

Furukawa came to see me as I was putting my shoes on to leave. He was courteous, but firm.

"Would you be interested in learning about the ki philosophy of health. . . ." he said as a statement rather than a question.

"Not today," I snapped and left without saying good-bye.

Mrs. Matsuura's prediction did not come true. Not only was I not in agony, in fact the pain had become so mild as to be easily tolerated. It now occupied the entire length of the leg down to the tips of the toes. However, it was no longer my constant companion and only thought. I could take mental leave of it and devote my mind and body to familiar pursuits. I began thinking fondly of Mrs. Matsuura. The fondness turned almost to love when, after the second week following treatment, the pain started leaving my body, seemingly flowing down the leg and out of the toes. Every day brought about two inches of relief, and I expected a full recovery in a fortnight. I regained my appetite and began looking at women again.

When I next saw Mrs. Matsuura, I thought it would be my last visit, and I was giddy with elation and gratitude. I talked a blue streak, hating to pause, wanting to fill every second of our short time together with fulsome praise of her. I repeated half a dozen times that I would be free of pain within two weeks without going through the agony she anticipated for me. I was boasting. I was childishly trying to show the woman who had done nothing but right that she had been wrong in this one thing. She listened quietly, holding my printout. At the end of the session she bowed but kept me before her with the look of her bright, black eyes.

"Listen carefully. The end is in sight, but it will not be easy. You have a wonderful body and have so far been a model patient. But you will not recover without the final reaction. You've healed faster than anyone I've ever treated, which means your reaction will be that much more extreme. Don't be surprised when it comes. Don't panic. Don't take medication. Don't fight it. Just ride it out for a few days, and you'll be fine."

"What's going to happen?" I asked anxiously. This reaction sounded ominous.

She sipped her drink and thought. "Who can say? You've been housing an illness for eighteen months, maybe longer. Toxins have built up, which have to be expelled in order for you to heal completely. Your body is building up to a purge. This is called *gedoku*. If you experience fever, stoke it, keep it raging so that it burns itself out quickly. Take hot compresses, as hot as you can stand, and hold them to the back of your neck under the skull. There's a nerve cluster on either side. That will keep the fever going and speed up the healing time. From today soak your feet up to the ankles in water as hot as you can stand. Twice a day, morning and night, four minutes each time. This will stimulate the nerves. The feet will be bright red when you withdraw them from the water. Pat them dry, and put on thick socks to hold the heat in. If you are in severe pain, soak your legs up to the knees. Come again when the gedoku is over."

"Can't I come when it begins?" I was only half joking.

She laughed merrily. "Act the man. No one can help you over gedoku. I would only set you back. Stop worrying and have some fun. Fun is the best health restorative. Have you been skiing yet?"

Gedoku began four days later. Fortunately I was at home, or I might have been carted off to a hospital by mistake. It was early evening. I lay on my futon watching a Clint Eastwood film on television. It was very amusing to hear Mr. Eastwood sneer in Japanese. It became him even more than English. He stopped sneering, however, when a deranged thug cracked his skull with the butt of a machine gun and stood over the prostrate hero sneering at him in Japanese. Moaning, Eastwood withdrew a knife that he had had the foresight to strap to his leg and stabbed the thug in the thigh. At that exact instant the outside of my left thigh began to twitch and tingle. The pain in my leg seemed to swell, grew to a vital maturity, and then began to move down the leg and out through the toes. I could feel the pain leaving me. It passed below my knee, then down to my ankle, then to the sole of my foot. I wanted to cheer. It was just as the pain was on the verge of departure that the sole of my left foot felt as if it were being gripped by a powerful, red-hot metal hand. It was being crushed and burned simultaneously. I was consumed by pain. A booming crash filled my head. I saw on the television that Eastwood had shot the thug with a portable cannon.

My foot grew hotter, the grip more viselike. I began having trouble breathing. My breath came out in stuttering bursts, and it hurt to inhale deeply. I could hear sneering in Japanese, but I could not make out the words. My ears were sizzling on the inside, and my head held only annoying static. I thought of getting the painkillers I had been hoarding since my visits to physicians. They had been saved meticulously and were plentiful. I fought against the urge. Nor could I have moved even had I really wanted the pills. I was sure my sole was being singed. I could almost smell burning flesh. I was shocked to see that the foot looked normal—there was no incandescent glow, nor was anything squeezing it. It was the most innocuous, coy foot I had ever seen, and I hated it for leaving me without the satisfaction of knowing why I was dying. For I was sure I was dying. Sweat was pouring off my chest and face, running into my eyes and mouth. I shifted quickly to wipe my face, and as I did, the pain and the heat and the deadly grip left my foot and lodged in my head faster than thought.

My leg, I realized, was pain free for the first time in almost two years. I was too sweaty to care. The pillows and bedclothes were drenched. Now that I could walk, I fetched two bath towels, but they were soon saturated and had to be wrung out constantly. I tried standing under a cold shower to relieve the searing heat, but it only became worse and gave me an unendurable headache. I thought of applying hot compresses to the back of my neck, but I was suffering enough. The prospect of even greater heat appalled me. I returned to bed with a bucket, into which I wrung out my towels.

The fire in my brain was worse than any pain I had ever known. I felt that I was hovering between madness and death. Mrs. Matsuura had advised me to ride out the pain, but the pain was riding me. It was the most unequivocal reality I had ever met. There was no denying it. One could only assent. Yet that got one nowhere. I covered myself with the towels and let them soak up the sweat.

This state of affairs lasted about four hours. I was delirious and aware that I was talking to myself. The television had long ceased transmission and was buzzing mindlessly. I blathered on, with no idea what I was saying. The bucket, which could hold five liters, was nearly full. I could not believe there was that much water in the human body. The heat subsided somewhat; I felt a breath of coolness on my cheeks and prepared myself for an end to pain. But the heat flared up as unexpectedly as it had subsided. It was now more intense, more concentrated at the top of my skull. I thought I smelled the roots of my hair burning. I decided to phone Mrs. Matsuura, have her confirm that this was, in fact, gedoku, and ask if my variety could be fatal.

I put out my hand for the phone, and, as in the case of my foot, the heat and pain leaped out of my head and into my belly. My guts turned over with a terrible groan, and I ran to the toilet to open the floodgate to endless diarrhea. It was milky-white liquid. I spent the remainder of the night, about five hours, sitting on the toilet urinating and defecating and sweating while my stomach burned and churned. I could not sleep. I could not stand. Each time I rose, I was seized by an irresistible urge to defecate.

By mid-morning the diarrhea had stopped, and the pain had become tolerable. I was running a low-grade fever and sweating mildly, but steadily. I phoned Mrs. Matsuura, told her exactly what had happened, and concluded that I was through with gedoku.

"Congratulations," she whished bouyantly. "You've passed through the first stage. You will have a pain in your groin, and when that passes you'll be completely better. Stay someplace today where you feel comfortable. Keep close to home and wait for the pain in the groin."

I thought I had climbed Mount Everest only to be told that I was still in the foothills. I was desolate, but also eager to try out my resurrected leg. Feeling weak and clammy, I defied orders and went to work. The retribution of diarrhea fell upon me at once, and I stood for two hours motionless over a squat toilet, testing the strength of my leg to the utmost. My atonement over, I went straight home, determined to live a blameless life.

In the early evening I felt as if I had been suddenly punched in the left groin. The pain from the blow swelled, and I could feel that the area was inflating like a balloon. There was, of course, no visible swelling, though the area had turned a mottled purple. The pain radiated out in billows from a point the size of a peppercorn, and once again I broke out into a heavy sweat. The area where the thigh joined the groin became so painful that bending the leg was impossible. I took down my *Complete Works of Shakespeare* and settled in for a long sweaty night. At the zenith of my pain, I felt that I truly understood Lear's madness and realized that Shakespeare, too, had once undergone gedoku.

The purge ended as abruptly as it had begun, almost thirty-six hours after the onset of pain. I was weak, fatigued, and confused, but I was pain free. My entire body had the congenial, forgettable quality of non-feeling that we associate with health. I was too spent to be elated. I had lost twenty-four pounds in thirty-six hours and weighed a pathetic 140 pounds, down from 184 pounds two years earlier. I had a ravenous hunger and thirst, and I longed to sleep for days. But I was a well man, almost three weeks to the day since Mrs. Matsuura had first treated me.

I fell asleep after the gedoku ended and slept nearly twenty-four hours. I resumed working at home, not venturing out too far, and ate in moderation four times a day for three days. The diarrhea persisted in a desultory way, and I decided to experiment. I drank a tumbler of Kaopectate on the second day, but it passed straight through me. My bowels returned to normal on the fourth day. I celebrated by taking a six-mile hike through the hills west of Tokyo.

The ground was thick with sodden leaves, which lay piled over the slippery, mucky paths. I was strangely aware of the soft sucking sounds my footsteps made. It was as if I had never before known the sensuousness of walking. I stumbled occasionally and shuddered that I might have undone Mrs. Matsuura's handiwork, but she had advised me to do vigorous exercise. As I walked on, I grew confident that my body had returned to its original durability. On the way home, when I was pleasantly tired, my left leg felt weak and listless, but that was to be expected after eighteen months of inactivity. I still tended to favor, needlessly, the right leg.

In the following days and weeks, in fact, for about eighteen months following gedoku, I felt an occasional tingling in the toes of my left foot. The tingling would be followed by a sensation of numbing cold. At first I worried that the cure had not been a cure and that I was relapsing into sciatica. Mrs. Matsuura told me to continue to soak my feet twice daily. By doing so, the sensation, though it did not end, came less frequently and grew shorter and shorter in duration.

Two weeks after I resumed my work, my life settled down to its accustomed routine. I returned to Odawara to have Mrs. Matsuura confirm that I was well and truly healed. This she did. I bowed deeply and thanked her profusely for healing my back. She was nonplussed.

"There was nothing wrong with your back," she said. Her hands fluttered around her chest for emphasis.

I knew better than to argue. "Well, my leg then," I corrected myself.

"Your leg was fine."

I protested. "But I had a herniated disc that caused sciatica."

"*Herniated disc* is just a term that explains nothing. Your vertebra twisted and pulled the nerve with it."

"What made my vertebra twist?"

"Sciatica."

"Do you mean I had sciatica before I had the twisted vertebra?" I was more than confused; I was baffled.

"Yes, of course."

From the start it had been obvious that our concepts of the human body and its functions were without common ground save that we both used the same criteria for discriminating between life and death. Stemming from this difference, she always had an awkward time trying to answer my questions, for they were, a priori, incomprehensible to her outlook and experience. Not that she treated my questions as second rate; rather, they were indicative of an alien mentality that she doubted she could ever convert to reason. My bewilderment elicited a tender explanation from her.

"Your vertebra did you a favor by hooking the sciatic nerve. Had it not done so, you really would have been in trouble. Your vertebra was trying to anesthetize you from pain."

I was beaten, and I knew it. Had she been anyone else I would have smiled wanly and edged out the door. Then I would have done a public service, such as erecting a sign outside her house reading "Beware! Lunatic within!!" But I was desperate to know what she had done, to get at least an inkling of what seemed to be the illogical and incomprehensible approach she had taken to restore me to full health. The other treatments I had undergone were logical and ineffective. This to me was right and just. Some things work, and some things don't. That her treatment had been illogical and effective struck me as paradoxical. It was out of the question that her success had been a matter of luck. She had diagnosed correctly from her first observation, and her prognosis had been too conclusive to admit that possibility.

I implored her to explain what she had done. I begged her mercy for my ignorance of the precepts of her technique. The fact that I acknowledged that her treatment had precepts pleased her. Perhaps conversion was, after all, possible.

She poured herself a cool drink from the pitcher that was always by her side and drank it slowly, ordering her thoughts. She was not a gifted expositor. She was used to communicating by active example and spoke in an awkward, telegraphic style. Her voice was low with a raspy edge to it that made it interesting.

"The printout indicated a twisted lumbar vertebra and loss of strength in the left leg. I felt your spine to check that the other vertebrae were aligned. Your spine and legs were normal, although your L3 vertebra was twisted to the left. It had clearly hooked the sciatic nerve. That wasn't important. The important thing was to find what made the vertebra twist. I looked at you on the floor. Two things were clear—first, that your body was crooked. Second, and more important, your outside left ankle was two inches higher than your outside right ankle. I recognized that as the problem. The area beneath the ankle had a great concentration of heat. The impulse running through the sciatic nerve was impeded at L3, but that was natural, given your condition. The impulse was far more obstructed beneath the ankle. That confirmed my opinion. There was a wide gap between your ankle and foot, which exposed a nerve cluster along the sciatic nerve.

"That was undoubtedly very painful. You began subtly to favor your right leg, which threw your body out of balance. The nerve cluster would certainly have become terribly inflamed and might have led to a loss of feeling in the foot if your vertebra had not twisted and hooked the sciatic nerve. It did this to dull your pain. It was acting on your behalf. Your pain was moderate compared with what you would have experienced had your body not taken this step. That's why I said you have a healthy, sensitive body.

"What I did was simple. I lowered your ankle, untwisted the vertebra, and then stimulated your body to heal itself as quickly as possible. I haven't been able to bring your ankle back to its original location. It's a gradual process. A few more sessions and it will be back in place. Watch."

She placed her thumb just under the left ankle and pressed lightly. The pain made my eyes water.

"That's it, right there. The culprit," she said, satisfied with her point.

"What caused my ankle to ride up?"

"Who knows? It's not uncommon. It's tough being an ankle. They're delicate creatures supporting a lot of weight. They twist, bend, get kicked, knocked, and abused without your even knowing it."

I had another question. "How did you stimulate my body?"

She wrote the Chinese character *ki*. *Ki* (or *chi*) is a common word in Chinese and Japanese, meaning energy or vitality or vital essence or life force. The word had become known in the West in the past ten years through the martial art Aikido, in which I held a black belt, and through acupuncture. I had always thought of ki as raw energy, a force of dubious power mainly used to overcome an assailant. Channels of ki are the basis of acupuncture, and needles are used to monitor and modify its flow. Mrs. Matsuura, however, had used only her hands, and although I had felt internal changes taking place when she touched me, I assumed they were the result of manipulation. In fact, the hardheaded, rational part of my mind refused to accept the notion of ki as anything more than an entertaining Oriental mystery that provided news filler on slow days. Mrs. Matsuura, of course, disagreed.

"What is the difference between a living person and a recently deceased person? Anatomically and physiologically there is none. There is only the presence or absence of ki. You may have your doubts, but the fact is that it exists. This is how I healed you. I sent ki up and down your spine and along your sciatic nerve to locate obstructions. I brought down your ankle with ki, I untwisted your vertebra with ki, and I've been stimulating your nerves with ki. The only time I didn't use it was when I pulled your legs out from under you. That was to restore your center of gravity. I'm a frail old woman. How could I possibly manipulate a man of your size using muscle power?"

My rational doubts notwithstanding, my body knew that it had never met a more forceful, more incisive pair of hands than Mrs. Matsuura's. My disbelief was dispelled two years later, when I saw a demonstration of Mrs. Matsuura's ki that so confounded conventional medical belief that I became an instant convert to the power of ki.

I asked, "Is that why your hands and fingers are so warm, because they're loaded with ki?"

That amused her. From the way she laughed I knew she would pull that line out in the lounge bar at the next ki practitioners' convention.

"Hot hands shooting bullets of ki into living bone and tissue," she giggled. "Maybe they'll take me to Hollywood to make an action film."

Furukawa came in, drawn by her laughter, and she related the joke. He took it with the studied gravity of a young man immersed in his life's work.

"Her hands seemed hot to you because your body is receptive," he said loftily. "Your ki absorbed hers."

Mrs. Matsuura calmed down enough to speak. "Some people I just can't work on at all. Their ki is too different from mine. I send them to another practitioner. Our ki gets along famously. I knew you were better after the first treatment by the way your ki reacted. It's possible to gauge a reaction by points along the abdomen."

I asked her for a last piece of advice, assuming that I would have to follow a strict regimen to prevent a relapse.

"Soak your feet up to the ankles every morning for four minutes in water as hot as you can stand. That will stimulate your nerves. Don't get too involved in your work. Moderate it with play. Get a girlfriend. Take a trip. Go dancing and keep active. You'll find that as a result of your treatment, your body is more sensitive to environmental stimuli than previously. Seasonal changes, humidity and dryness, things like that. Have treatment on a regular basis. There are plenty of good practitioners in Tokyo, most of them better than I. Find one you like for a monthly treatment, especially this time of year, as winter gives way to spring. Ki is for promoting and maintaining health. Its curative powers are secondary. My job is to help you fulfill your capacity for health. Some people can be very healthy; others can never be healthy. Still, it's best to be as healthy as you can. My guess is that your body will want to continue with ki work."

I regained my lost weight in four months, one of the most pleasurable experiences of my life. Meals were neither gargantuan nor lavish, but they were frequent. Mrs. Matsuura monitored my weight gain and pronounced it good. Friends and colleagues, astounded by my swift recovery, asked for introductions to the miracle worker. Dr. Shibata went to see Mrs. Matsuura about a persistent kidney ailment. He had been unsuccessfully treating himself for years. She healed him in twenty minutes and advised him to pay more attention to his posture. He was never again bothered by it. Two of his physician friends with chronically bad backs went to see her, were healed, and promptly denounced her as a charlatan. Her methods, they said, violated every known medical practice. A woman I introduced was cured of infertility, she told her friends, and I was quickly on my way to becoming a sort of medical pander.

I saw Mrs. Matsuura once or twice a month. My ankle had been perfectly repositioned, and I always felt energetic and amiable after a session with her, qualities that I was sorely needing in larger doses as I worked to recoup the financial losses incurred by being for so long out of commission. I was tired and feverish after each session and had come to look forward to sleeping and sweating on the return train trip, taking it as a sign of health. I refrained from bathing and drinking liquor for twenty-four hours following a session. Heat and liquor relax the body and make it easy for it to lapse back into its bad old ways, she explained. Give yourself twenty-four hours for the treatment to set in and the muscles to adjust to their new configuration; then drink in the bath if you like. My toes still tingled with cold from time to time. She assured me this was in the nature of things. The nerve was still settling down. My right thigh swelled up and became painful to the touch. Marvelous! she exclaimed. The perfect response to a change in season from cold to warm. I could do no bodily wrong. Had I been hit by a bus, she would have pronounced me fitter than before I was hit.

I was becoming the mascot of her practice. She praised my body unstintingly to others and frequently pointed me out as a model of Health Through Ki. People with headaches, backaches, sciatica, infertility, circulatory ailments, and whatnot would crowd round me and ask to hear my story. I was the "before and after" photos advertising a wonder-working bodybuilding course. Sciatica would never again kick sand in my face. My auditors were confirmed in their confidence in Mrs. Matsuura and encouraged in their determination to see their courses of treatment through to the end. Some women, preoccupied with fashion and thrift, went so far as to ask if Mrs. Matsuura had made my hair curly. One of her treatments was half the price of a permanent wave.

Furukawa and I became friendly once I showed interest in ki health philosophy. He indulged my ignorance at length, explaining and demonstrating until I had come to grips with the fundamentals. He instructed me in exercises to be done at home that would keep me in good health. He insisted that in time the exercises would enhance my sensitivity to external stimuli, that my five senses would expand to full capacity. There was certainly a change, but I cannot say that at the time I was aware of dramatically enhanced sensitivity. What did happen was that I became more sensitive and susceptible to Mrs. Matsuura's treatment, and I developed the tendency to yawn frequently and to catch colds and get over them quickly. Mrs. Matsuura was pleased. Furukawa was boyishly delighted, as if I had given him a gift. I, on the other hand, complained excessively, only to be told that yawning is a sign of health and that colds are essential to the body's self-regulating mechanism. I ought to cherish every cold that came my way, soak my feet, place hot compresses on the back of my neck and over my sinuses, and think how healthy my runny nose and watery eyes were making me.

I learned that Mrs. Matsuura was eighty years old by overhearing a chance conversation. To a man distressed about growing old, she said, "And you only seventy-five. You should be ashamed of yourself. When you reach my age, then you'll have the right to complain. And I won't listen because I'll still be five years older than you."

She wore her age lightly, like a comfortable garment. I had long ceased thinking of her as old because of her astonishing vigor. She worked six hours a day, taking off every fifth day to go shopping. Some days were seven or eight hours long, for she never turned anyone away and gave each person as much time as was necessary for effective treatment. Her memory was prodigious. She talked as she worked, inquiring after husbands, wives, children, school events, vacations, treatments of two or more years past. She always showed an interest in her patients more intimate and intense than social convention demanded. Passing thoughts and trite observations were locked in her memory to be taken out at a moment appropriate to invigorating the patient by her regard for him and his life.

She seemed to have a running feud with her hair. I never saw her but that it had not been newly misshapen and recolored. She preferred having her hair chopped rather than cut. She said she was so ugly that it did not matter what her hair looked like as long as it was short. The unearthly colors were accidental, she confessed. She was seeking a color that she could visualize but had not been able to concoct. Hence the unending and fruitless color changes as she went from experiment to experiment. Patients, especially those whom she had healed, fulsomely complimented each new color of the month. I, too, finally joined the chorus. She was genuinely upset when I did; she thought I had more taste and intelligence.

A year after I first met her, the organization's head office retired Mrs. Matsuura, and the Odawara practice was taken over by Furukawa. Mrs.

Matsuura showed no sign of disappointment and encouraged her regulars to give Furukawa their patronage. She had postcards printed announcing her entry into private practice and sent them as a matter of courtesy to every person in her files.

She worked out of her home, keeping the same hours and charging the same ¥3,000 (then $20) per visit. Her house was small but comfortable, with a tidy garden. It was an easy walk from the organization's clinic. Her husband was also a practitioner, three years younger than she. Their treatment rooms were separate. Mrs. Matsuura's was by far the larger of the two, as befitted her larger practice. Her husband took pleasure in his wife's superior medical skills and frequently recommended intractable cases to her. Most of the time he kept out of sight in his work area. Occasionally I would see him in the kitchen, head in hands with paper and pen before him. I learned later that he wrote poetry and composed problematic essays on the need to integrate the fundamentals of atomic physics into ki health principles. He had earned a master's degree in health science from the University of California extension course in this subject. The next two years passed uneventfully between Mrs. Matsuura and me. I saw her regularly, devotedly. She looked forward to my visits. There developed not so much a friendship as a warm rapport. The friendship came later, when she found out what a good son I was.

Chapter 2

Sciatica is a devilish thing. Now exorcised, my dispossessed sciatica sought a new host and soon found one in my mother, Marty. Its trip from Tokyo to Miami took eight weeks.

My mother bore the twinges and jolting flashes for four months, then had X rays and CAT scans taken. The results were demoralizing. She had no discs to mediate between her lumbar vertebrae. The vertebrae were rubbing harshly against each other, irritating the sciatic nerve. Hence the keen backache that accompanied the sciatica in her right leg. The only remedy was an operation to fuse the vertebrae together into one friendly solid mass. It would have to be done sooner or later, the physicians declared. Why postpone the inevitable, suffering intense pain while undergoing ineffective alternative therapy? They made her a keepsake of the X rays, the implacable proof upon which they based their diagnosis and prognosis. She carried them from alternative therapist to alternative therapist, hoping that someone could read them in a way that would admit the possibility of nonsurgical relief. No one could.

After three years of fruitless pilgrimages to acknowledged centers of Alexander technique, Feldenkreis technique, acupuncture, and osteocranial treatment, she reached the limit of her physical endurance. Unlike me, she grew fat on sciatica. Seeing her radiant and bulging, friends and colleagues disbelieved her claims of chronic pain. She got little sympathy. Softhearted intellectuals used words such as hypochondria to explain her condition; others cloaked their nastiness in the "unpleasant truth" style of bogus frankness and called her a goldbrick. She began having crying jags, and through tears, agreed to come to Japan to let Mrs. Matsuura have a crack at her.

The winter of 1984 was Tokyo's worst in fifty years. As if chronic pain were not misery enough, snowdrifts, frozen roads, interrupted train service, and a home heating system incapable of coping with blizzard conditions added to Marty's torment. Thrice weekly trips to Odawara were planted with so many obstacles to health and comfort that finding the Matsuura house safely took on the nature of a perilous quest. And as with all quests, the desire for rich rewards at journey's end became all-consuming.

The Matsuura house was warm and bright, a pleasing contrast to the bitter conditions of Tokyo. One side of the house, that facing the garden, was floor-to-ceiling sliding-glass windows. The Pacific sun warmed the hallway that was Mrs. Matsuura's waiting room. Patients sat with their backs touching the glass, absorbing the warmth. Carpeting had been laid, obviating the need for thick socks. Since her retirement, the majority of Mrs. Matsuura's patients were women. Modesty and decorum prevailed in the Matsuura house; there was no longer lounging or sleeping in the waiting room. Mrs. Matsuura kept the white paper sliding doors closed when she worked on women, and Marty was unable to get a glimpse of her until it was her turn to be seen.

During the three years I had been visiting Mrs. Matsuura regularly, I had become charmed by her outsize personality and deeply respectful of her abundant energy. It amused me, therefore, to read in Marty's expression upon being introduced to the old woman an unblemished copy of my own first impression. The tininess of the woman and her appalling hair clearly did not inspire confidence. Mrs. Matsuura's winter wardrobe—a thickly padded hip length jacket worn over heavy woolen purple slacks—was so bulky that it emphasized the smallness of her features. Marty was used to being manipulated by large, robust practitioners of both sexes and saw little good coming from a woman half her size.

Mrs. Matsuura read Marty's weight distribution printout with intensity but gave no sign that anything was amiss. Marty offered her the trove of X rays and CAT scans, but Mrs. Matsuura refused to look at them. "In orthopedics, X rays are like mirrors," she said. "They show the seeming of things, not the truth of things. They are useful only to those who have been trained to diagnose without touching."

She made a quick, tactile appraisal of Marty's body, first the back, then the front. She circled several of the figures obtained from different positions on the printout and showed them to me. "Remember these. They are what we'll change." After two minutes of further touching and stroking, she pronounced Marty in excellent health. It was a classic performance. Pulse, reflexes, brain, internal organs, metabolism—all sound. Fat? She's not fat in the clinical sense. She's just heavier than she's ever been. Her body has changed, but what's unusual about that in a woman just turning sixty? Forget about it. Hers was an open and shut case; just two sessions were necessary.

My mother had not come all the way to Japan in the dead of winter for such easygoing optimism. She blinked repeatedly, stymied for something to say. Perhaps, she said finally, I was interpreting poorly. Perhaps I had failed to communicate the gravity of her ailment. Perhaps Mrs. Matsuura really would like to look at the X rays. Mrs. Matsuura did not look up from Marty's body. "Your mother is a worrier. Tell her to relax," she said.

Mrs. Matsuura had a new assistant, a young mother of two. She was short, stocky, and hearty, helping Mrs. Matsuura with the muscle work that had been Furukawa's task. She had no intention of becoming a practitioner. She admired Mrs. Matsuura and wanted to be with her, learning easy health-maintenance techniques she could use on her children. Mrs. Matsuura had been a teacher too long to let an eager ear escape her and had the assistant present when she made her telegraphic diagnoses.

"Body slants to left. Toes point inward. Prominent hip bones. Pelvis spread widely. Hmm. High center of gravity. Relies on brain rather than emotions. Thinks a lot. Tendency to self-absorption. Energetic. That's it." Marty considered these unsystematic remarks meaningless. The old woman had not even mentioned her spine. I knew that the remarks were meaningful, but only to Mrs. Matsuura.

91

Chapter 2

Interpreting was becoming precarious. I had to appease the curiosity and anxiety of the one without wasting the time of, and irritating, the other. Marty was not receiving step-by-step satisfaction and adopted an attitude of blind faith tainted by a smidgen of skepticism. It was only when Mrs. Matsuura knelt over her and began to work that my mother had the inkling that something might, after all, come of the treatment. Mrs. Matsuura's first words startled Marty.

"You're a very bad sleeper. You don't look forward to sleep. You don't enjoy sleeping."

"She's right! How did she know that? Ask her," Marty demanded. It is a point of pride with her that she is one of history's worst sleepers.

"It's right there, in her body," Mrs. Matsuura replied gruffly, like an artisan who knows her job. She spent a short time feeling the culprit lumbar vertebrae but did not work on them. Surprisingly, she concentrated her attention on the sacrum and coccyx, which she sweated over for ten minutes. She first placed her palm on the coccyx and gave ki for about five minutes. She then had her assistant straddle Marty, place her thumbs on either side of the coccyx, and exhale deeply, telling Marty to exhale with her. As they exhaled in unison, the assistant bore down on her thumbs and remained like that until breath was exhausted. As she bore down, the assistant gave ki through her thumbs. Mrs. Matsuura felt the results by hand and, after making some slight adjustments herself, ran her hands over Marty's spine for a few minutes, checking for obstructions on the neural line.

She then moved to the toes of the right foot. She tugged and tweaked, pressing her thumb above the ankle. Marty felt short bursts of pain, but nothing unbearable. This lasted a quarter of an hour. She cradled Marty's head in her arms and pushed a spot above the right breast. Marty gasped with pain. Mrs. Matsuura pushed another point on the rib cage just below the left breast. That point, too, was tender. She gave that point and a second point on the rib cage a dose of ki and then depressed the former point hard. There was no pain. "You'll sleep soundly for a while," she told Marty.

Last, she had Marty sit on her knees and knelt behind her. Placing her hands on Marty's temples, she gave ki to the brain for a full five minutes. She then declared my mother officially cured. "The first session is the cure. The second session will be to make the cure permanent. Come back in a week. One more quick session and you can return to America and get on with your life. Won't that be nice?" She motioned to her assistant to fetch the next patient.

Marty did not think that would be nice. First, she did not want to wait a week. Her time in Japan was limited, and daily treatments were imperative in every other therapy she had tried. She had me impress on Mrs. Matsuura that she wanted lots of treatment. Then there was another, pithier reason. The idea that she could be healed in two sessions was outside the bounds of probability, and it demeaned her suffering and devalued the expense of coming to Japan. It was as if, having endured so much, it would be mortifying to be healed before the eleventh hour of her stay. Mrs. Matsuura should be monitoring her condition moment by moment, completing the course of treatment with a vital adjustment at Narita Airport as my mother boarded the plane home.

The two women dickered while I played Honest Broker. Three visits a week was finally agreed upon, the next session to be in three days.

Mrs. Matsuura was resigned. "I suppose since she's come all this way, it would be cruel not to give her what she wants," she said. "But honestly, two sessions will do it. Never mind, I'm enjoying your filial piety [in Japanese, *koko*]. You know the saying, 'When I finally got around to wanting to do *koko*, my parents were dead.' This is your chance to do *koko* that means something."

I asked for instructions to pass along to Marty. I received the predictable duo: Soak the feet and get out and have some fun. "This is for your benefit," Mrs. Matsuura added breezily. "You can tell your mother or not, as you like. Her condition is much less serious than yours was. She's not going to have a big reaction or a violent gedoku. She's got a sensitive system, so a reaction will come quickly, but the course of healing will be gradual. Age, of course, is a factor, but so is the temperament of her body."

On our way to the station, Marty slipped on a patch of black ice and came down hard on her coccyx. She began to cry, not from pain but from frustration and fear of having undone Mrs. Matsuura's work. She wanted to return at once for an adjustment, but I persuaded her to go home and assume Mrs. Matsuura's treatment could not be vitiated by a thump.

That night my mother had a short, sharp bout of high fever and nausea. She vomited twice. The treatment had taken. Marty was not convinced. She had more confidence in an itinerant flu bug than in Mrs.

Matsuura. Her back and leg pain were worse in the morning and worsened yet more day by day. I confused and irritated her with my delight at her aggravated condition. She, too, expected instant relief from pain, or at least a diminution of pain. Increased pain worried her. She began to mutter darkly about Mrs. Matsuura's "arrogance" in ignoring the X rays. She lay in bed for two days, alternating between ruminating and reading Malcolm Lowry's *Under the Volcano*, which, perversely, cheered her up.

I was heartened by the optimism she showed as we set out for her second session. She was determined to be plucky, and what a mercy that was. A violent storm interrupted train service to Odawara, and it took three hours to get there. Only a handful of locals had come for treatment that morning, and Marty was Mrs. Matsuura's last session of the day. "Just as well. This is going to be heavy duty," she said cryptically. "I'm liable to be exhausted at the end of it."

Just how intense it would be was plain when she had Marty strip to her bra and panties. Even the most critically ill patients were treated in their street clothes or long underwear. When Marty was lying faceup on the tatami, Mrs. Matsuura called her assistant and pointed to my mother's hip bones, the day's objective. She then had Marty stand in front of a full-length mirror.

"Too open," she said to the assistant, not unlike an art critic sniffing at a statue. "Look at your own hips in the mirror. You can judge how far hers have spread."

She squeezed Marty's fleshy waist and bust, rubbing the skin like a garment inspector appraising cloth. "Tell your mother I'm going to give her a new waistline and push her bust up. Have her look in the mirror now and tell her to remember what she looks like."

Marty was told to resume her position on the floor. The assistant sat on Marty's left and Mrs. Matsuura on the right. Mrs. Matsuura placed her hands on Marty's hip, stretched her arms, and rounded her shoulders, presenting a passable likeness of a flying buttress. "Do this to keep her from sliding off the mat," she told the assistant. When the assistant had braced herself, Mrs. Matsuura placed her hand flat on Marty's protruding hip bone, closed her eyes, and breathed deeply for a minute. Marty and the assistant, with a total weight of about two hundred and fifty pounds, were pushed backward off the mat.

Mrs. Matsuura complained to me, "She has to be kept from moving.

Get over there and help hold your mother." I took up my position. Mrs. Matsuura recommenced and pushed the three of us backward. I spread out facedown on the tatami, feet flat against the back wall, arms outstretched, palms on my mother's left hip. Marty was pushed toward Mrs. Matsuura.

"That's fine," the old woman said, and went to work for the third time. The power welling out of her hand was intense, a numbing pressure. My back was the first to feel it, then my arms, which began to quiver from tension, and, last, my legs. The strain on my knees caused them to bend, and I had to concentrate to straighten them.

Mrs. Matsuura had hit her stride. She had summoned up an armada of ki, sent it sailing off with an intense effort, and could now maintain its progress with a minimum of concentration. She began to gab about current events and the cost of rice. Wasn't it a scandal? The government was actually hoarding rice to keep prices up. Soon they'd be paying farmers not to plant. Can you imagine? Well, I never!

I heard a distinct, ominous creak—a horror movie, ancient dungeon door being pried open noise—and raised my head to see what made it. My mother's hip had moved. Mrs. Matsuura was turning it inward, slowly, toward the left hip. The creaking noise ceased, and the bone seemed to be turning easily. My mother was in no pain but felt a strange sensation. The tip of the bone continued its upward, arclike movement and then stopped. Mrs. Matsuura stopped her babbling and became serious once more. She closed her eyes and breathed deeply, exhaling slowly and intensely. The hip gave a sound like ice cracking and began to move again. Mrs. Matsuura went back to her news roundup. She tried to include me and turn the monologue into a conversation, but I had no surplus strength. Holding my mother firm took all my energy, and I grunted politely at appropriate intervals. Nor was Marty the least bit interested in giving an opinion on world affairs. She seemed hypnotized by the sensations going through her.

Twenty minutes after she had begun, Mrs. Matsuura had the hip where she wanted it. She took Marty's pulses and felt along neural pathways. Then she rested, haggard and breathless. Fifteen minutes later, the left hip received the same treatment as its twin, and with the same result. When she was satisfied, she had Marty turn over, and she gave ki to the entire lower back. Mrs. Matsuura rested another quarter of an hour and then went to work on the waist. She kneaded the flesh like dough with

95

both hands for a couple of minutes. Next she pushed the flesh inward and upward for a few minutes more, finally holding the waist in position and giving it ki. The same was done to Marty's bust. At last, Mrs. Matsuura went over Marty's entire body with her hands, gave her neck and head a long and intense dose of ki, and fell back, utterly spent. Her body looked more birdlike than ever. I saw her then as I saw her the first time we met: a frail old woman who looked in need of being carried to bed. The session had lasted almost two hours.

Marty stood up, and Mrs. Matsuura appraised her handiwork. She was pleased. And so she should have been, creating a near masterpiece out of unpromising material. My mother had a distinct waist, and her bust rode girlishly high on her chest. The hip bones were no longer thrusting outward but seemed to be conversing. My mother could hardly believe it. She kissed Mrs. Matsuura's hands.

"Anyone could have done it," the old woman said, flustered, but without false modesty. She believed herself to be no more than a common foot soldier of the ki organization's army. There were career officers above her. "There's no more to be done. That's it. If she exercises regularly, I guarantee my work for the rest of her life. If she does no exercise, I can give it only twenty years," she said and sipped her cold drink.

"When she says I'm all better, does she mean structurally?" Marty asked.

"What other way is there?" replied Mrs. Matsuura. "She is physically perfect and can go home." But Marty reminded her of the bargain they had struck, and Mrs. Matsuura could look forward to receiving her again in two days.

"I can work on her sleep, lower her blood pressure, get her to relax, give her some pointers on posture—odds and ends. Tell her to get out and have some fun. The worst is over. It's all downhill from here. She's youthful in constitution, and she should work at having a good time. If it doesn't come easily to her, I'll take her out and teach her myself," Mrs. Matsuura promised and showed us the door.

The experience, even to me who had been initiated into the ways of ki, had a supernatural quality. Mrs. Matsuura was more godlike than human. Or if human, then she was the earthly conduit of a higher power. My mother and I were so astounded by Mrs. Matsuura's performance that we could talk of nothing else for two days. And yet, with the passage of years and the death of Mrs. Matsuura, I have trouble conjuring up the vividness of those original impressions and begin to question my memory. Not that I doubt that my mother's hips were repositioned by ki alone. The fact that my mother was healed and continues in good health testifies to the event. Rather, I wonder if I do not exaggerate or mystify a commonplace event made remarkable by a lack of familiarity with ki. Mistrusting my own memory, I have had my mother confirm the exactness of my account. We reconfirm each other's memory of the event. I have since seen demonstrations of the power of ki performed by other adepts. I have no doubt of its power and value. The point, the sadness, is that even with firsthand experience, I have backslid into the narrow and predictable confines of Western medical thinking. The once real becomes improbable and, should I talk to enough medical people, impossible. But, as I say, my mother and I both have our health, and that should be real enough to dispel my ungracious doubts.

We returned to my flat, and I had high hopes for a ki reaction in Marty. There was none. I recalled that the first session had been curative, hence the reaction, and that the second had been preventive, hence the absence of a reaction. Still, I was disappointed. The next day broke sunny. The past three weeks, especially the week since Marty had arrived, had been relentlessly grim hours of unremitting wind and frost. The sunshine could be construed as a break in the weather, perhaps a turning point. To call it a watershed in the annals of meteorology might be going too far, but after weeks of sunless skies, it was easy to be excessively impressed. From that impulse it was a single, blithe step to construing a parallel between the new, improved weather and my mother's new, improved condition. It was an omen.

The worst was over; Mrs. Matsuura had said so herself. It would be warm and sunny with intermittent birdsong. Marty would progressively improve. In fact, with a good night's sleep behind her, she may already be over her pain, I thought with the dim-witted optimism of half-wakefulness.

Marty was whimpering in the next room. She was unable to move for the pain in her hips, legs, and back. Breathing was painful. What had Mrs. Matsuura done? What had gone wrong? How could she be structurally well and have such towering pain? I tried to explain vibrating nerves, but her pain was not of that sort, she said. It was a muscular or bone pain that seemed to radiate out of the body's very structure. I phoned Odawara, but Mrs. Matsuura had already left the house, presumably to chide the local rice growers. Marty lay in a teeth-clenched, stoic silence that day. I maintained a sympathetic vigil nearby.

The obvious reason for her condition occurred to neither of us. Thus can the fear engendered by the interplay of pain and sympathy make fools of the most willing to be cured. Marty and I actually gasped at our own obtuseness when Mrs. Matsuura said the next day, "It took twenty years for your hips to open up. I closed them in less than an hour. Don't you think it would be strange if they didn't hurt?"

She had Marty get on the weight-distribution measuring machine and compared that printout with the former. It was clear from the figures that there had been a major change in Marty's body, but I did not understand how to interpret the figures and could only assume that change had occurred in the way Mrs. Matsuura had anticipated. Mrs. Matsuura found the results satisfying and explained in that murky way of hers just why this was so. I interpreted word for word, and my mother, like me, was none the wiser.

Mrs. Matsuura performed what was to become the standard treatment for Marty now that she had been "cured." After a quick finger walk down the spine to count the vertebrae and ascertain that individual vertebrae were aligned, Mrs. Matsuura gave ki to the hips, the lower spine, the coccyx, the head, and the solar plexus. She found a slight tendency to arthritis in Marty's right hand, what is commonly called a trigger finger and gave ki to the spot. She investigated Marty's "sleep points," which had been so painful at the first visit, and found them responding well to treatment. Marty reported sleeping longer and more deeply despite the pain.

Throughout the treatment Mrs. Matsuura kept up a steady monologue, most of it in praise of Marty and her body. She praised her youthfulness, her vigor, her courage in coming to Japan for treatment. Her compliments were simple and effective. She praised artlessly, as if she had been blind too long to so many wonderful things and could not suppress her spontaneous exclamations of delight. Marty was not used to being praised by people in the healing profession and wondered if Mrs. Matsuura were not covering up some tragic news with pleasing words.

Marty began to have good days, when the pain left and she was able to walk freely. We took brief trips out of town on those days, and she would return home in the evening bursting with satisfaction and eager for another foray. Inevitably, the pain would return, more intense and debilitating than before. At these times she would take to bed, disconsolate. She alternated between optimistic faith in Mrs. Matsuura and deep pessimism. Mrs. Matsuura continued to encourage her to ride out the pain and to get out of bed and have fun. "How can I have fun when I'm in agony?" Marty complained to the old woman.

"I'll help you. We'll go to an *onsen* [a hot spring resort] together. Next week is my husband's eightieth birthday, and we're going to an onsen for a party. Why don't you two come along? It's a beautiful place. The bath is outdoors, carved out of the natural rock with an ice-cold waterfall plunging into the far end of it. We'll have a good time, and that will make you feel better and speed your recovery."

During the week of waiting for the party, Marty's pessimism prevailed, and she felt convinced that Mrs. Matsuura had not structurally cured her. She had me arrange with Dr. Shibata to take X rays of her lower back the day before we were to go to the onsen. Dr. Shibata was not an orthopedic surgeon, but he had taken an interest in Marty's case. He was a true believer in the talents of Mrs. Matsuura, but studying Marty's X rays and CAT scans made him dubious that anything other than a laminectomy could relieve her pain. He agreed to take new X rays for comparison with those she had brought, in order to ascertain what changes Mrs. Matsuura had wrought. Comparison revealed no change at all.

Marty was devastated. Dr. Shibata tried to comfort her by saying that not even Mrs. Matsuura could accomplish the impossible; hers was an intractable case that manipulation could not dent. His words gave little comfort. Marty looked at the old and new X rays and was speechless. They were identical. The lumbar vertebrae had not changed in the least. A cure could not have been effected.

Even I felt crushed. I was stricken by the total collapse of my mother's morale. There was nothing I could offer by way of explanation or defense of Mrs. Matsuura. X rays may well show only the "seeming" of things, as she had said, but it was a powerful seeming, especially in light of the word "structural" that both my mother and Mrs. Matsuura had agreed upon.

I had never seen my mother give herself over to utter despair. We rode home in silence and ate in silence. My mother took to her bed in silence, and I could think of nothing cheering or hopeful to say. Meeting

Mrs. Matsuura for the first time had filled me with a wild and groundless optimism; it was like meeting a stranger who, one feels certain, has good news. Now, in the face of my mother's despair, I was bereft of hope. Marty was disinclined to go to the onsen the next day, but I persuaded her that she should. She packed both sets of X rays.

The hotel was large and elegant. The hot spring was indeed as Mrs. Matsuura had described it: a large pool cut out of living rock facing a high, tree-lined bluff down which poured a frigid waterfall. The water seemed to burst and sing as it hit the rocks along its course. Icicles clung to projecting rocks on either side of the falling water. There was a small wooden hut where we undressed for bathing. It was dark in the early evening. Small lamps hidden behind rocks and clumps of bushes cast just enough light to guide one through the enormous pool. The water was hot and slightly sulfurous. Steam rose in wisps or billows, according to the movement of the water. Marty relaxed and stretched out. I urged her not to speak to Mrs. Matsuura about her problem that evening, but to let her get on with the birthday party. It would be more suitable, I said, to question her at the time of treatment the following morning. Mrs. Matsuura had offered Marty a session before we left the onsen. Marty concurred but was on tenterhooks. The beauty of the surroundings and the heat of the bath had done much to lighten the heavy darkness of her emotions. I found myself regaining my accustomed confidence in Mrs. Matsuura and felt that I could easily contain myself until morning to get to the bottom of the so-called structural change.

Mrs. Matsuura had invited ten people besides me and my mother. These people were locals, and would return to their homes when the festivities concluded. Only the Matsuuras and the Fromms would stay the night. My mother and I had been given a large suite overlooking a secluded garden. Mrs. Matsuura had already paid for the room. The charge was more than she would receive from my mother for the course of her treatment.

The atmosphere of the Japanese-style banquet room was homely and lively when we entered and were shown to our places on the tatami. Marty was given a seat of honor, next to Mrs. Matsuura. The hotel management, maids, serving girls, and other personnel were making a grand to-do over the old woman. At first I thought that she was a regular guest whose lavish spending had endeared her to the hotel staff. In fact, she had treated and cured everyone working in the hotel for ailments one could only guess at. They were clearly honored by her presence that evening and elevated the usually attentive Japanese service to a level I have never experienced before or since.

The guests, too, had more than just friendship binding them to Mrs. Matsuura. The spontaneous, effusive outpouring of gratitude to the woman was moving. My mother and I felt more than a little churlish for entertaining doubts about her competency, and I decided to broach our matter lightly and get it over with before the festivities began. It would be a pity to have anything in mind that would detract from the pleasures of the evening.

I said, "My mother had X rays of her lumbar vertebrae taken and there was no structural change to them. Are you surprised?" I said this as blandly as if I were telling her about a minor purchase we'd made, and she replied just as blandly.

"I'd be surprised if they had changed. I never touched her lumbar vertebrae. They're fine. Why change them?"

These were deep waters. Marty and I were so shocked at this that we were satisfied to leave our further questions until the morning. Marty complained that I had botched the translation of the word *structural* or had asked the wrong question or something and was enlivened. As enigmatic as Mrs. Matsuura's reply was, it left the door open just enough for hope to sneak back in.

The food was brought in a little at a time, small dishes containing delicate morsels of fish and vegetables, each prepared and displayed differently. A toast was proposed, then another and another. The eating continued, and each person formally introduced her- or himself seated. Most people were middle-aged, but there were two teenagers and an elderly physician who had sculpted the artworks decorating the Matsuura home.

In the middle of dinner, a drunken strolling player wandered into the room, saw that he had made a mistake, and attempted to stagger out. He had been asked to perform by another party at the hotel, but what with all Japanese doors looking alike and he too drunk to notice even had there been a difference, he lurched into our soirée. He was dressed in the weirdest costume I had ever seen, looking like a hooligan Kabuki performer, with wild shabby clothes, a desiccated wig, and outlandish makeup, asymmetrically applied. The guests begged him to stay and entertain. He accepted at once. He was not as drunk as he seemed. I thought his drunkenness was an act to get himself into the room, a piece of Japanese tact. He probably did not have clients waiting for him in another part of the building but was too artistic and proud to go room to room begging for work.

His song and dance was a ludicrous burlesque of famous Kabuki scenes, and he spiced his songs with impromptu lyrics suited to the birthday occasion. He performed for twenty minutes, had a drink while guests threw questions at him about his life and background, and quickly became too "drunk" to answer. Then he staggered out of the room. He had other parties to crash that night.

Mrs. Matsuura was enchanted by his performance. She laughed till she cried and marveled how a drunk could maintain his balance so well. She called for the manager to ask how a person in such a costume could sneak into the hotel. The manager replied that "he used to work here" and that some of the guests found him amusing. "He was wonderful," Mrs. Matsuura declared and told the manager to give him money. The manager, by a slight inclination of his head and a lowering of his eyes, indicated that he had.

Each person in attendance that evening performed for the entertainment of the Matsuuras. One woman did a dignified traditional dance while her daughter accompanied her on the *shamisen*. She had changed into an elaborate kimono and wig for the dance, which unfolded slowly but came to a rousing conclusion. One man turned out to be an amusing storyteller, throwing in so many puns and double entendres that I gave up interpreting. Marty had to be content with enjoying his silly voices and the laughter his story provoked. She then entertained the guests with a mental exercise designed to conjure up their fondest memories. Finally, Mr. Matsuura rose and recited his poetry.

He was a short, stocky man, dressed in a somber kimono. He looked years younger than his eighty. I was prepared for elaborate, even recondite classical verse, but he had prepared festive limericks for the occasion. When the laughter subsided, he recited a poem he had written for his wife. It was affectionate, with a sexually suggestive pun at the end. Mrs. Matsuura was embarrassed by the public display of affection but as happy as a schoolgirl at the sentiment.

The party broke up at about 9:30. Taxis were called to take the other guests home. The Matsuuras disappeared the moment the last guests had been seen off. Marty was tired and went straight to the suite. I had another long, fulfilling soak. When I returned to the suite, I found Marty restless to speak with Mrs. Matsuura. She slept poorly that night, but relaxed somewhat in the bath the following morning. Trying out various interpretations of Mrs. Matsuura's latest words on the state of her back, she was becoming frustrated and repetitive.

The Matsuuras had a room on the ground floor next to the garden. We went there after leaving the bath and found Mrs. Matsuura alone. Having finished breakfast, she was contemplating the garden's wintry sunshine. She had a remarkably tranquil look. She said she was not in the mood to do therapy that day. Marty no longer needed her in any case. Her husband's therapy was better suited to Marty's present condition, she said. However, she agreed to talk with us until he came out of their private mineral bath. Once again she declined to look at the X rays.

"They show only bones. But you have more than bones there. You have muscles and ligaments that move the bones, and they don't show up on X rays. Besides, I don't know why you had your lumbar vertebrae X rayed in the first place. That wasn't your problem."

"But the X rays show that there are no discs between the vertebrae," Marty argued gently.

"So what?" Mrs. Matsuura was unperturbed. "I know that. I also know that the vertebrae have fused perfectly. The nerve isn't interfered with in the slightest, nor is the movement of the lumbar vertebrae. Your muscles are seeing to that. No, the problem was in your sacrum and the bones of the coccyx. They were higgledy-piggledy. I straightened them. I don't suppose you ever had X rays taken of them."

Mrs. Matsuura took Marty's abashed silence as "no." She sighed and looked thoughtful. "I suppose I should have explained, but so few people ask or are interested in the process, just in the results. I'll tell you what I did, and that should put an end to your worries and questions.

"Your printout indicated trouble in the coccyx. I confirmed this by running ki down the spinal cord. There was no obstruction in the lumbar vertebrae; however, the passage of the ki through the coccyx was obstructed. The health of the coccyx is directly related to sleep habits, and so I assumed yours were poor. And so they were. Your sleep points, if you remember, were extremely painful. It did not take a miracle to figure out that not only were you a poor sleeper but you did not even want to go to sleep. That's why working on your sleeping was a great part of the cure.

"Next, your head shows hyperactivity, and your body shows inactivity. You are dominated by your head, which is also related to your sleeping problem, but that doesn't concern us here. What concerns us is that you lead a sedentary life, hardly ever exercising your back muscles in a meaningful way. The muscles grew loose and flabby. They didn't support your spine, which sank lower and lower, causing the hips to splay and the coccyx to get even more out of alignment. The human body always seeks health. You may not be aware of this, but it does. Your coccyx, out of alignment through poor sleeping, would have tried to realign itself in some way. However, your spine was putting so much weight on it that it couldn't maneuver. Imagine trying to get out of bed and stand up straight only to find you've got a crushing weight on your chest. It was the same thing.

"The first thing I did was raise your spine to give the coccyx some breathing room, and then I straightened the coccyx. I could feel the ki flowing without obstruction through both legs and knew that your sciatica was over. I next pushed your lower-back muscles up and closed your hips to hold everything in place. That's what I mean by structural. It was simple, though tiring. You're cured. Now you can wait for the nerve to settle down and for the pain in your hips to go away. My husband can give you exercises to strengthen your back muscles. He can also give you an exercise to do alone at home to promote your sleeping. With a modicum of deep sleep and effective exercise, I promise you will never be troubled by sciatica again, at least not of this sort."

Mr. Matsuura did as advertised and had Marty run through a variety of bending and stretching contortions that made her grimace as she did them. She later asked Mrs. Matsuura if she had to continue those exercises, or if she could substitute others for them. "The exercises he showed you are designed for people like you who hate exercise and rarely go out. You can walk, swim, climb mountains, bicycle, ski, do whatever you like. The body is meant to be used. But use it regularly and in moderation. You can't get a year's worth of movement in two weeks of violent exercise. Walking a thousand miles in a week will not suffice for the year. Just walk a little every day, and that will be enough."

While the four of us waited for the taxi to take us back to the

Matsuura home, Mrs. Matsuura had additional words for Marty, who was irritating her by trying to pay for our share of the evening. "It was a pleasure for me to treat you, and I'm eager to do it again. Think of it as part of your treatment. You have very little faith in your body. It inclines toward health, and you have to encourage it. That means forgetting pain and immersing yourself in pleasurable activities. You know that the surest way to free yourself from anxiety is to become immersed in some activity that takes your mind off yourself. In Japan they have people copy sutras, and that seems to do it. Well, the same sort of thing is necessary for physical illness. When I tell you to go off and have fun, I mean it seriously. I hope last evening suggested possibilities to you."

Marty was cheerful on the train home, but still skeptical. "Do you really think I'm better?" she asked me.

"Yes."

"You really think what she said was my problem?"

"Yes."

"Do you realize someone might have cut me open only to find that there was no reason to cut me open?" That thought pleased her. She likes saving time and money. "Call Dr. Shibata and ask what he thinks."

I was inclined to ignore what anyone but Mrs. Matsuura thought. The relation of sleep to the coccyx would be hard for Dr. Shibata to grasp, as would be her contention that the lumbar vertebrae were healthy. I demurred, but Marty pressed me. Dr. Shibata was, not unexpectedly, pessimistic.

"She might be right, but if she is, it goes against all common medical practice. I can't imagine anyone seeing an X ray of her lumbar vertebrae and not wanting to hospitalize her immediately. Mrs. Matsuura undoubtedly knows more about the working of the body than most physicians, but if she pulls this off, I will call it a miracle." Six months later Marty's last pain left her, she became healthier and fitter than at any time in the past ten years, and Dr. Shibata pronounced it a miracle.

Marty continued to languish in bed, suffering from chronic pain during the final two weeks of her six-week stay in Japan. We saw Mrs. Matsuura regularly. She was overbooked on one visit, and Marty had another grueling session with her husband in the next room. However, Mrs. Matsuura helped Marty sleep better and lowered and regulated her blood pressure, as in the case of curing her sciatica, through ki.

The old woman became tearful and sentimental at Marty's last visit. "I'm going to miss you. Your son has been a model of koko, and that's always wonderful to see. You're very lucky to have him taking care of you. I wish I could see you together more. Mothers and sons make beautiful pairs." She looked sad rather than glad at the sentiment. She seemed to find farewells awkward and embarrassing.

"You have a healthy body. Don't avoid exercise. Force yourself. Eat as much as you like, but only as long as the food tastes good. When you stop enjoying it, stop eating—even if you still feel a bit hungry. It's the sign that you've eaten enough to satisfy your bodily need. And for goodness sake, have fun! Not occasionally, but make it an integrated part of your life."

Marty cried and thanked her profusely. The paper doors were open, and the barren garden with patches of early March snow and puddles of water lay before us. The scene added to the melancholy of the farewell. Marty became sentimental and fulsome in her gratitude to the old woman.

"I did very little," Mrs. Matsuura said. The Japanese take compliments poorly, especially Mrs. Matsuura's generation. Even so, she really did seem to believe that her powers were limited, hardly worth the time and expense it took to come to see her from Tokyo, much less from Miami. "You are healthy, even though you don't yet feel it. I simply helped your body regain the health it sought. Anyone could have done it."

Marty took the old woman's bony hands and asked if she would like a gift. Money? Clothes? Jewelry? Something vain and tempting? Mrs. Matsuura was flustered. She ran her fingers through her short, colorful hair and rubbed her forehead. "What a waste on an old crone like me. That sort of stuff is for the young and beautiful. I have enough money to live. Money and such are vain and tempting only to vain, tempting people. I'm not one of them."

Marty continued to press her to accept something. In the end, Mrs. Matsuura smiled slyly. "There is one thing I would like. I don't know where Miami is. I don't know what it's like. But I would if I had soil from there. Send me a box of earth from Miami. Earth is what is wholesome and lasting. It's what binds people. If I have soil from you, I will always have you. You will live here with me. I don't want to spend you or wear you. I want to live with you and show you to others. Send me soil."

"But soil has no value," Marty protested. "I can send it and give you another gift as well."

"I will show you the value of soil," Mrs. Matsuura cried and scrambled crablike over the tatami in search of something from a low shelf. She pulled out a small box and removed a satin bag. Inside the bag was the seed of a sequoia tree I had given her two years before as a souvenir of my summer vacation in California.

"Just think," she said, "this tiny seed produces the largest, oldest living things in the world. Some are as old as Japan, and like Japan, they come from the soil. When I show this to people they are amazed. There's a postcard of a sequoia tree to go with it. Look at that! Isn't nature incredible!"

Marty gave up trying to enrich Mrs. Matsuura with worldly goods and resigned herself to bestowing the earthly upon her. Mrs. Matsuura bowed low at my mother's generosity and then went to work on the next patient. Marty left to hobble home and await the miraculous.

This story has an amusing postscript. As soon as she arrived back in Miami, Marty went to the beach and collected three pounds of sand and a dozen shells, which she promptly packed and sent to Mrs. Matsuura. She went to the expense of sending the package by air freight. She phoned to inform me that Mrs. Matsuura would be receiving her gift within ten days.

A month passed without any news of the package. Marty grew anxious and made a second trip to the beach as a backup measure. I was sure the package had been lost in the mails and was at the point of telling this to Marty when Mrs. Matsuura's assistant phoned. She had been contacted by the Japanese Customs Service about a package from Miami. Knowing nothing about it, she called me.

The package had arrived safely at Narita Airport. Customs inspectors shook the box, heard the sand rattling and slithering inside, looked at the Miami postmark, and concluded that someone had sent a four-pound box of cocaine to Odawara. They opened the package, and the sand and shells fell out. They analyzed all of it for traces of the drug but found none. Baffled by the nonsensical gift and still hoping to smash a drug ring, they phoned Mrs. Matsuura's house for information. The sand and shells were now in a plastic bag awaiting collection. I went to Narita Airport, explained the gift to the doubting agents, and duly delivered it to Mrs. Matsuura. The story did not amuse her. She thought the customs officials had been very high-handed. It reminded her of the worst days of the war. I explained as best I could, but I could not make her see the humor of the story. She did not know what cocaine was.

Chapter 3

It was late September, 1984, six months after my mother's return to Miami. Odawara was luxuriating in warmth and abundant foliage. Small cars carrying large surfboards on roof racks were jamming the roads. Knots of tourists clutching guidebooks formed around the train station. Like basking turtles, they stretched their necks for a glimpse of the tower of Odawara Castle. Up in the hills, persimmons were ripening in orange clusters against deep green leaves. The roses in the Matsuura's garden were gearing up for their second blooming of the year. They were tall and spindly, carelessly tended. The large sliding windows facing the garden had been removed to create a long, narrow veranda. Three matrons awaiting treatment sat on the edge dangling their stockinged legs over the side. They discussed their ailments in a sympathetic undertone. Mrs. Matsuura sat inside on the tatami, grumbling.

"Two more people asked me to give them shells." She shook her head. She had arranged the sand and shells in a small glass case, which was displayed prominently in an alcove. "Everyone who comes here sees the shells and wants one. People are so grasping! Sometimes it makes me want to despair."

I asked, "Have you given any away?"

"Certainly not!" She sounded like an Orthodox rabbi asked if he would like ham and eggs for breakfast. "Your mother sent them to me. They're all I have to remember her by."

In the six months since I had seen her, Mrs. Matsuura had begun displaying mementos of gratitude given by her patients. Perhaps it would have been unkind to display my mother's sand and shells and not the gifts of others. I had the feeling she was gearing up to some kind of retirement; that she was putting the entire cast on stage as a prelude to the grand finale. In any case, the room had become small and cluttered. Most of the gifts were handmade, many showing considerable skill: paintings, origami, collages, sculptures, fans, and a few very tacky room deodorizers disguised as lace picnic baskets. "Look at all this," she said, indicating the gifts with a sweeping gesture. "I'm very lucky to have such thoughtful and generous friends."

We sat on our knees, talking. Her posture was as erect as ever, but her shoulders had begun to sag. She seemed to have aged in the past six months. She was wearing a drab duster. The light shapeless garment had neither neck nor sleeves and stopped at the knees. Mrs. Matsuura looked smaller than ever. Her skin was aged and seamed. Large liver spots had formed on the backs of her hands. Her face was more gaunt and her eyes set deeper than I remembered from a short four weeks before. The skin on one cheek was darkening like a gathering storm. She had let her hair grow out, then cut it off to within an inch of the skull. She had not bothered to dye it, and it was a lackluster gray. I thought to inquire after her health but, perhaps fearing to hear the worst, did not.

She worked on me with her customary speed and economy of movement. She checked the alignment of my vertebrae, blood pressure, internal pulses, flow of ki, and left ankle. After ten minutes she said, "There's nothing for me to do for you. You're in perfect health and don't require treatment today. I'll have my assistant refund your money." This started a ridiculous argument. I begged her to keep the money as the price of the diagnosis, while she insisted on being paid only for services rendered. She began to slap her forehead, which I knew as a sign that her patience was at an end.

"I've brought a map of the world," I said, unfolding a pocket map I had cadged from an airplane. I spread it on the tatami. She was dumb-struck at the distance from Miami to Tokyo.

"It's hard to believe your mother found me. She had to come from way over there, using planes, trains, buses and then walking up that hill to get to this very room. What an achievement!"

"It wasn't easy, but it was worth it."

"Yes, it was. I learned a lot from her. She was a very interesting woman."

"I didn't realize you two spoke together."

"Her body talked to me. We had lots of chats. I can find out more about a person's personality and character through ki than if the person talked for days. Ki never lies or deludes itself. Your mother is energetic, aggressive, and impatient. She is led by her head rather than by her emotions. The two are usually kept separate in her case. You and she have different, but compatible characters."

The talk turned to her husband's health and then, quite naturally, to her own. "It's as good as can be expected at my age," she said matter-of-factly. "I should have been dead years ago, you know. Bad blood pressure and circulation problems. If it weren't for ki treatments and that nice doctor you met at the party. . . . He treats me occasionally, and I treat myself daily."

I looked at the arrayed gifts. "Do you ever think of retiring?"

She smiled. "I am retired."

"You don't act it."

She took a drink from her constant companion. Her movements were blunt and mannish, in contrast to the exquisitely feminine form of Japanese that was her second nature. "I'm a stubborn old woman. Why should I sit on my hands all day when I can use them to help people?" She pointed to the matrons sunning themselves on the veranda. "I've started urging people to see Furukawa. He's very good, a full-fledged practitioner. I'm proud to have him as my successor. Look, I've got more mementos than patients now. I see only four or five people a day."

She removed the glass case from the alcove, and inspected the shells individually. "A most wonderful gift," she sighed. "I'm very lucky to have known you and your mother. I've never heard of such devoted koko. And you're not Japanese." Her face became grave, and her eyes grew blank.

"Do you have children?" I asked.

She did not answer. She sat like a well-worn pebble, staring emptily at the sand and shells. The assistant had been standing to the side of the paper doors listening. She entered noiselessly and motioned me to leave.

"Sensei had two children. One died," she whispered.

The toes of my left foot began to tingle and throb as the weather grew cold. I phoned Mrs. Matsuura for advice. She told me that my ankle had probably come slightly unstuck, but it was nothing to worry about. She advised me to soak my feet and do my ki exercises daily. She told me to hold on to a bar or lean against a wall with my right arm and kick my left foot down and to the left in such a way that my ankle would "snap." Finally, she gave me the name of a local practitioner. She phoned him and discussed my history, and he lowered the ankle in a single session.

I spent very little of the winter of 1985 in Japan, only three weeks. I returned to Tokyo from California on April 7 and phoned the Matsuura house the next day. My mother had given me a gift to pass on to Mrs. Matsuura, and I had a hunger for another treatment from her. It had been almost five months.

A stranger answered the phone. She was sorrowful and not altogether coherent. Mrs. Matsuura had suffered a massive stroke three days earlier and was in the hospital. More than that she was unable to tell me.

I canceled my business appointments and went at once to Odawara to see Furukawa, who explained what had occurred. The stroke had been so sudden and devastating that Mrs. Matsuura had not been expected to live. Her death seemed a foregone conclusion, but by morning she had regained consciousness. The physicians thought that her mind had been irreparably damaged. Furukawa thought otherwise. He had taken the measure of her ki and was sure her mind was intact. However, she was paralyzed from the neck down. She was presently listed in critical condition with little hope of survival.

I took a taxi to the hospital, a new and uninspiring building on the outskirts of town. The architecture and placement defied the environment, appearing starkly oblivious to the passage of days and the change of colors. Not even the spring sunlight and budding green of fields and trees could warm its bleakness. I imagined that all the patients were cold.

Mrs. Matsuura shared a room with six other women. Her bed was by the window overlooking the parking lot and was besieged on all sides by floral displays and baskets of hothouse fruit. Half a dozen local matrons whom I recognized sat outside in the hall, waiting to be of use.

She looked unchanged, the slightest thing in the world. Her t hardly disturbed the flatness of the covering sheet. The bulge wa ger than a broom handle would make. She smiled weakly when near and spoke my name. Her eyes still had their dark radiance, but n their penetration. They seemed resigned to seeing rather than looking.

Mrs. Matsuura had never been a model of elocution, and she was now extremely difficult to understand. She spoke with the same old-fashioned respectful female language she always used, but so softly that I could hardly hear.

"I'm so happy. I'm so lucky. Thank you for coming."

I thought her mind had gone into what the Japanese delicately call a state of "ecstasy."

"Happy? Why?" I asked stupidly.

"To have you here. To have known you and your mother. I have known so very many people. I have so very many friends. I'm a very lucky person. I'm very happy."

"I love you," I said.

Her right hand began to twitch violently under the sheet. "Pull it off!" she said. Her hand was shaking and shuddering, jerking spasmodically as if it had one more burst of ki to give. She looked at it calmly, as if it were a remarkable bird that one could admire but never possess. The fluttering hand bore no relation to the woman who smiled approvingly at it. I took her hand and felt it pulsate and quiver.

"Put my drink in it," she said.

There was a sealed plastic bottle topped by a straw next to her bed. I put it in her hand. She managed to grip it, but that was all. The liquid sloshed noisily inside. She sighed and asked me to put the straw in her mouth. "Oh, that's good, that's very good," she said with feeling. "This is an encouraging sign." She indicated her right hand. "I want to be back at work again soon." She closed her eyes, and tears welled at the seams of the eyelids. "You said you loved me," she whispered.

"I do love you. My mother loves you. All who know you admire you and love you." I took her hand again and tried, fruitlessly, to steady it. She opened her eyes. She looked like a dainty death's head. "I don't deserve it, but I'm so very happy." She closed her eyes and was quickly asleep.

I spoke by phone with Furukawa daily. On the tenth day of Mrs.

Matsuura's hospitalization, he informed me of a change. "They're moving her. She refuses to sleep and shouts at the top of her voice during the night. She's disturbing the other patients, and the doctors don't know what to do with her. There's a small convalescent hospital about twelve miles from here that has an onsen attached to it. She's been taken off the critical list and is being sent to the other hospital ostensibly to undergo rehabilitation."

"Do you think she's capable of rehabilitation?"

"I think her will has grown stronger and her body remains unchanged. She's brought herself back to life by willpower and has recovered her mind using willpower. But she realizes that she will never be able to bring her body around, and so she sits up nights shouting. I advise you to see her as soon as you can. She frequently asks after you."

The new hospital was small and built of red brick, sitting among paddies lime-green with rice seedlings. Low green hills rose gently nearby, and Mount Fuji loomed white and impressive in the distance. I paused to take in the panorama. Mrs. Matsuura was in a large ward, once again by the window—this time with a warm, long-familiar view. There were a few flowers in a vase and no fruit. Thousands of origami cranes hung gaily from the curtain railings around the bed, traditional bribes to divinities to have one's prayers answered.

Two women were in attendance. One I recognized as the maid from the onsen where Mrs. Matsuura had given her husband the birthday party. She was deeply chagrined. "Sensei has been in a bad mood since she came here. I hope she'll speak to you." Mrs. Matsuura lay inert. Her eyes were fixed on the ceiling, her expression cold and determined. She did not acknowledge my presence. The maid spoke to her as if she were a pettish child. "He's come all the way from Tokyo to see you. Aren't you going to be nice and say hello to him?"

Mrs. Matsuura lay as rigid as a stick. "I told you. I'm sure she hears us," the maid said loudly enough to be heard at the reception desk. She took Mrs. Matsuura's lack of reaction as a snub. "Please don't be angry with her. She's become willful and stubborn, but I suppose that's to be expected from someone in her condition."

The woman left noisily, and I sat in a hard chair by the side of the bed, looking at Mount Fuji playing hide-and-seek with the clouds. I walked around the ward, dumbly reading the charts of the other four patients. None of them looked like a candidate for rehabilitation. It

made me sad to see them. I sat back down and stroked Mrs. Mats'
arm. It was cold and lifeless. I wondered if she had long to li\
became inexpressibly sad. I was on the point of leaving when her head
turned slightly and she looked intently at me. She asked, "Is that woman
gone?" Her voice was barely audible.

"Yes."

"Good. I'm glad you've come. I wanted to say good-bye to you. I've
decided to die. I don't want to be a useless thing."

I began to cry. I stammered, "How?"

"I have decided to die, and I will die." She clamped her jaws shut and
turned back to face the ceiling.

I talked to her, certain that she heard and understood, for five minutes. I spoke firmly, but softly in order not to be overheard by the atten-
dant in the hall. I thanked her for my health, reminded her of certain
incidents that had amused us, and told her that I had decided to attend
training classes at the organization. Sitting by her withered arm, I spoke
into her ear that she was the most decent, most admirable, most capable
person I had ever met. My emotion raised my volume. The maid heard
my voice, assumed that Mrs. Matsuura was conversing with me, and ran
in to be greeted by disappointment.

"I don't know what's gotten into Sensei," she said as she saw me to
the elevator. "She's made it this far on willpower alone, and just when
things begin to look a little better, she suddenly gets into this black
mood."

Mrs. Matsuura had made the decision to die. She could not bear to
be a useless object confined beyond the margin of life. She lusted for
health, and death was the only truly healthy state left her. She lusted for
an active role to play, and only death afforded her the opportunity. She
would not be passive, dying by degrees, while she still had the power of
choice. She had exerted herself to regain the strength to make a conscious effort to die. She chose to die as she had lived, wilfully and with
no regrets. She remained in the position I last saw her. Her clamped jaws
could not be pried open. An intravenous drip, rigged up as a last-ditch
effort to save her, was rejected by her body. She was dead in two days.

The Buddhist wake was delayed three days in order to give mourners
time to arrive from distant parts. Some came from as far away as Hok-
kaido and Okinawa. Furukawa undertook to manage the arrangements

and was helped by Mrs. Matsuura's assistant. Mrs. Matsuura's magnetism had not ceased with her breath. At least eight hundred mourners attended, the line snaking from the house down the hill. They waited patiently, talking in subdued voices in the way I had watched hundreds wait for treatment at her hands. No doubt they were describing what she had done for them, how she had healed them.

A black-and-white-striped canopy had been erected over the driveway. Furukawa stood at the head of the receiving line, directing people to the guest books. Each mourner signed the book and left an envelope containing cash, usually $75 to $100 per person, to help defray the funeral expenses. I left two envelopes, one from myself and one from my mother. Furukawa was, as always, composed and helpful.

He said, "I don't suppose you'll be coming to Odawara anymore."

"You never know. I might have a relapse and come to see you for old time's sake."

He laughed. "Go into the house. The family have asked for you to sit with them."

The little house was filled to overflowing. Mrs. Matsuura's "clinic" was reserved for the immediate family and relatives. A cushion on the tatami near the altar had been set aside for me. The room held Mrs. Matsuura's earthly remains. They surmounted a tier of shelving on which a nursery-full of white chrysanthemums had been placed. In the middle, toward the top of the mums, stood a larger than life-size black-and-white photograph of Mrs. Matsuura. It was a head and shoulders shot, taken at least ten years before. She was wearing a formal kimono and looked kind and unassuming. One could only guess the color of her hair on the day the photo was taken.

An altar had been erected at the foot of the mums, and three Zen priests entered and sat before it. One was middle-aged, the other two young. They looked blithe and carefree as they chanted the sutra, rather sloppily I thought. The smoke and fragrance of incense wafted about the room, mingling with the monotonal chant and dissipating in exiguous wisps. The line of mourners was passing slowly through the garden. The sliding windows had been removed from the runners, and a small altar stood just in front of the veranda.

Industrious gardeners had wrought an overnight miracle. Plants, vines, and bushes flowered in the lambent late spring air. A tiny pond and battery-powered waterfall stood where I had last seen a weed patch.

A path of white gravel guided the mourners through the garden and back out to the street. Each person would stop for a moment at the veranda and gaze indoors silently and solemnly at the photograph shining before him or her, then move on.

It was a hero's funeral. Not even the formality and precision of the Japanese could quell the emotionality of the event. No one cried or wailed; the family, especially, were composed. But hundreds of mourners gathered out of no reason other than gratitude. This is unusual in Japan, where business ties and social obligations are the prime forces behind large-scale funeral attendance. No one owed Mrs. Matsuura anything except her or his health. The plain people had come out in force to pay their last respects to a healer of genius.

Perhaps the finest tribute to Mrs. Matsuura was the unintentional one paid by a fellow practitioner. Eighteen months after she had last treated me, I found someone who, by his status and reputation within the association, was unusually adept at the art of healing. He ran his hands over my body for a couple of minutes and then said thoughtfully, "There is something remarkable about your ki. It's a sharp, eccentric sort of ki. It reminds me very strongly of a sensei who passed away not long ago, Mrs. Matsuura of Odawara. Did you ever have any treatment from her?" Her ki, her willpower for life and death, live on in me. I carry the life force of a willful little woman from a seaside city of Japan, and carry it, thanks to her, in good health.